Germany 1848–1914

Bob Whitfield

Series Editors

~~Martin Collier~~

~~Erica Lewis~~

Rosemary Rees

H E I N E M A N N   A D V A N C E D   H I S T O R Y

Heinemann Educational Publishers
Halley Court, Jordan Hill, Oxford, OX2 8EJ
a division of Reed Educational & Professional Publishing Ltd
Heinemann is a registered trademark of Reed Educational & Professional
Publishing Ltd

OXFORD MELBOURNE AUCKLAND
JOHANNESBURG BLANTYRE GABORONE
IBADAN PORTSMOUTH NH (USA) CHICAGO

First published 2000

10-digit ISBN: 0 435327 11 9
13-digit ISBN: 978 0 435327 11 8

05
10 9 8 7 6 5

Designed and typeset by Wyvern 21 Ltd

Printed and bound in Great Britain by CPI Bath

Photographic acknowledgements

The authors and publisher would like to thank the following for
permission to reproduce photographs:
AKG: p. 48; Corbis: p. 150; Corbis/Bettmann: pp. 33, 118, 124;
Hulton: pp. 12, 15, 29, 62, 102, 114; Michael Nicholson/Corbis: 32, 71,
113.

Cover photograph: © Mary Evans Picture Library

CONTENTS

How to use this book v

AS SECTION: NARRATIVE AND EXPLANATION

Germany 1848–1914
Introduction 1
1 Germany in 1848 3
2 The 1848 revolutions 14
3 Germany after the 1848 revolutions 25
4 The unification of Germany, 1862–70 35
5 Politics in the German Reich, 1871–9 50
6 Economic and social change, 1871–90 61
7 Bismarck's anti-socialist campaign, 1878–90 69
8 Bismarck's foreign policy, 1871–90 75
9 The fall of Bismarck 86
10 Germany under Wilhelm II, 1890–1914 89
   AS Assessment: Germany 1848–1914 107

A2 SECTION: ANALYSIS AND INTERPRETATION

Germany 1848–90
Introduction 115
1 Why did the German revolutions of 1848 fail? 117
2 Why was German unification achieved through
   Prussian victory? 127
3 How united was the German Reich? 143
4 How successful was German foreign policy,
   1871–90? 157
5 What was Bismarck's legacy? 168
   A2 Assessment: Germany 1848–90 173

Bibliography 181

Index 183

HOW TO USE THIS BOOK

This book is divided into two parts. The AS part on Germany 1848–1914 attempts to explain what happened in Germany during that time. The text gives the student detailed information and some explanation of causes and consequences. The summary questions at the end of each chapter will challenge the student to use the information to analyse, prioritise and explain the key features of the subject.

The A2 part covers the period 1848–90 but is more analytical in style and focuses on a number of key questions. Students who are intending to use the A2 part will need to read the relevant chapter of the AS part beforehand. For example, those studying the relative importance of the various factors leading to German unification will need to read the earlier Chapter 4 which outlines the process by which unification was achieved. The A2 part can also be used by AS students who wish to extend their understanding of the subject.

At the end of each part there are assessment exercises. These have been based on the new AS and A2 specifications. Guidance is given on how students should approach the different types of questions.

AS SECTION: GERMANY 1848–1914

INTRODUCTION

Revolution
In 1848 Germany, which was at that time a collection of 39 separate states, experienced a number of revolutions in many parts of the country. The revolutionaries tried to force their rulers to allow greater political freedom, more representative forms of government and the unification of the separate states into one Germany. By 1849 the revolutionaries had been defeated and across Germany the kings and princes regained their power. The revolutionaries' dreams of a united Germany appeared to be as far from realisation as ever.

Change and continuity
By 1914 Germany had been united into a single *Reich* (Empire). This Reich had a constitution that established a *Reichstag* (Imperial Parliament) which was elected by all adult males. Germany in this period had undergone more change – political, social and economic – than any other country in Europe; many of the aims of those who led the revolutions of 1848 would appear to have been achieved. The political changes, however, had been brought about not through popular pressure but through a process of 'reform from above'. One state, Prussia, had united Germany under its leadership through a series of wars between 1864 and 1871. The constitution, which was then introduced for the new Reich, despite making concessions to demands for a parliamentary system of government, recognised the King of Prussia as the sovereign power within the state.

Challenges
After 1871 the Reich grew in military and economic strength to become one of the great powers of Europe. There were, however, many challenges to be faced.

- There were many Germans who opposed the unification of the Reich under Prussian domination. Religious differences, traditional loyalties and the presence within the Reich of non-German minorities continued to divide the people. The challenge for the government was to integrate all these groups into a single nation.
- Social and economic change brought new tensions into German society. The most serious opposition to the monarchical system of government came from the Social Democratic (socialist) party, which, from the late 1870s, was gaining support from workers in the growing industrial areas. With its revolutionary ideology the SPD appeared to threaten the very survival of the Reich.
- The Reich had been established through Prussian military victories, especially those over Austria in 1866 and France in 1871. Once established, however, the long-term survival of the Reich depended on Germany remaining militarily powerful and on its ability to neutralise any future threats from these or other powers.

Bismarck

During the period 1862–90 one man, Otto von Bismarck, dominated German politics. His role in bringing about German unification and the extent of his success in coping with the challenges facing the Reich after 1871 are matters of debate among historians. What is clear, in light of subsequent developments, is that his very presence over a period of 28 years brought a sense of stability and continuity to Prussian and German government.

Wilhelmine Germany

The period 1890–1914 is usually referred to as the Wilhelmine period because, according to many historians, it was characterised by the 'personal rule' of the Kaiser, Wilhelm II. During this period the strength of the main opposition group, the Social Democratic Party, increased until by 1912 it was the largest party in the Reichstag. To meet this challenge the government tried to unite all non-socialist political parties behind it (*Sammlungspolitik*) through a policy of overseas expansion (*Weltpolitik*). Neither of these strategies was successful and by 1914 there was a sense of crisis pervading the German government.

CHAPTER 1

Germany in 1848

Germany in 1848 consisted of a patchwork of 39 independent states of varying sizes and importance. The two largest states were Austria and Prussia; Austria was at the centre of a large empire covering territory in Germany, Italy, Hungary, Poland, Czechoslovakia (then known as Bohemia and Moravia), Croatia and Slovenia. With such vast resources at his command the Austrian Emperor and his Chancellor (Chief Minister) Prince Metternich were able to dominate Germany. There were a number of medium-sized states such as Bavaria, Wurttemberg, Saxony and Hanover. Finally, there were many small states such as Brunswick, Anhalt, Nassau and Hesse-Darmstadt. All of these states were ruled by kings or princes who each jealously guarded their own power. Since 1815, however, all German states had been linked together through the **German Confederation**.

REGIONAL VARIATIONS

The German Confederation covered a wide area near the centre of Europe. Within such a large area there were inevitably variations in traditions, culture, society and economic development. The north and west tended to have more industrial development than the south and east (although the area of Leipzig and Dresden in Saxony was an exception to this rule). The north was mainly Protestant in religion whilst the south was mainly Catholic. Rulers of states in the west, such as Baden and Wurttemberg, allowed their subjects more political freedom than did rulers in the north and east, in states such as Mecklenburg and Saxony. Although Germany did not divide neatly into clearly defined geographical regions, we can see that northern Germany was very different from the south, as the east was different from the west. Rivers played an important role in marking the boundaries. The dividing line between

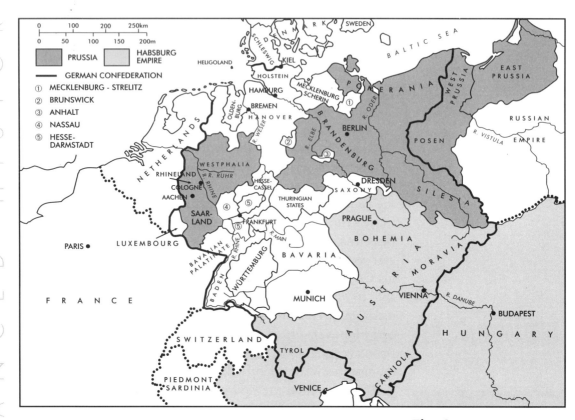

The German Confederation in 1848.

northern and southern Germany was along the line of the River Main, a tributary of the River Rhine; that between eastern and western Germany was roughly along the line of the River Elbe. With such wide differences in the lives and experiences of the German-speaking people, and with travel around this large area still relatively difficult, it is not surprising that the majority felt that their first loyalty was to the state in which they lived rather than to the idea of a German nation, a phenomenon known as **particularism**.

CONSERVATIVE FORCES

Germany had changed very little since 1815. Although there were some Germans who wanted to see greater political freedom and a united German nation, the forces which existed to preserve the status quo were far too strong. The most powerful of these conservative forces was the Empire of Austria.

KEY ISSUE

Particularism. The division of Germany into many different states led people to identify with the state in which they lived and its ruler, rather than with the concept of a German nation. The rulers themselves were determined to protect their own independence. These narrow, local loyalties were known as 'particularism'.

Austrian Empire

The Austrian Empire had been created in 1807, to replace
the medieval **Holy Roman Empire**. German princes had
owed allegiance to the Holy Roman Emperor; even though
this was no longer the case after 1807, the Austrian
Emperor still had enormous prestige and influence among
German rulers. Since 1835 Austria had been ruled by the
Emperor Ferdinand, although day-to-day control over
policy and administration was in the hands of the
Chancellor, **Prince Metternich**. Metternich devoted his
energies to the preservation of the status quo throughout
the Empire, Germany and across Europe. In his eyes, a
monarch was ordained by God to take sole responsibility
for the country's government; and a monarch's main
priorities were to unite subjects in loyalty to the crown and
to preserve order. Metternich distrusted intellectuals who
put forward ideas of individual freedom and people's
rights. In his eyes these people were dangerous and
irresponsible and should be suppressed.

Metternich as Chancellor. Under his direction the education
system of the Empire was strictly controlled, newspapers
and pamphlets were subjected to official censorship, and
spies and secret police officers reported on the activities of
people who were suspected of subversive activities. Through
Austrian leadership of the German Confederation,
Metternich was able to persuade the other German rulers to
apply the same policies in their own territories. During the
1840s, however, there was increasingly bitter rivalry within
the Austrian government between Metternich, who had
responsibility for foreign affairs, and Kolowrat, who was in
charge of home affairs. This rivalry began to paralyse the
government of the Empire; censorship became inefficient,
police control weakened and opposition began to develop.

The princes

Other German princes were also powerful defenders of the
status quo, since any change would inevitably weaken their
power. Within their own states they were the hereditary
rulers whose coronations had conferred on them absolute
powers to direct their governments. Not all German
princes ruled in the same way. The rulers of Bavaria,
Baden, Wurttemberg, Hesse-Darmstadt and Saxe-Weimar

had granted their subjects constitutions which allowed for the election of representative assemblies (parliaments) but these parliaments had no real power. Constitutions were, in any case, the free gift of the monarch; they did not guarantee any individual rights and they could be withdrawn at the whim of the ruler. By contrast, the rulers of Brunswick and Hesse-Cassel were notorious for their oppressive and tyrannical rule. Each of the rulers sent representatives to the Bundestag or Federal Diet (Assembly) of the Confederation where issues which concerned all German states were discussed, but, with Metternich's support and encouragement, they viewed the Confederation as a means of preserving their power and their independence, not as a body which would promote German unification.

The aristocrats

Equally conservative were the aristocratic landowners who still had many of the powers and privileges which had been acquired by their medieval ancestors. In Prussia, the *Junker* aristocrats owned vast estates which they ruled almost as if they were their private kingdoms, controlling the administration of justice and local government. At a national level within Prussia, the Junkers occupied all of the important command positions in the army and the civil service. Here again there were differences between east and west. In the western states aristocrats had smaller estates than their counterparts in the east and the peasants had more independence.

The peasants

The vast majority of the German population (75 per cent) lived in the countryside and worked on the land. The medieval institution of serfdom, by which the peasants were obliged to perform services and pay dues to the landowners, had been abolished in Prussia and the south German states but still survived elsewhere. In the west most peasants owned their own farms but most plots were too small to support a family and peasants were mainly poor, especially in times of bad harvests such as that of 1847. In the east, although the serfs had been freed in 1807, they still owed money to their landowners and, with agricultural wages being very low, they struggled to free

KEY INSTITUTION

The Federal Diet. Otherwise known as the Bundestag, the Diet was the Assembly of the German Confederation. It was made up of ambassadors from the German princes whose first priority was to protect their own power. The Diet met at Frankfurt, although there were only sixteen plenary sessions in the whole history of the Confederation.

themselves from debt. Among the poorest and most depressed peasants were those of Mecklenburg in the north, where poverty and ignorance went hand in hand. It has been said of the peasants of Mecklenburg that they were so restricted in outlook that they had no 'Fatherland', only a 'father village'. Metternich well understood the implications of keeping the peasants in this state when he said: 'The labours to which this class – the real people – are obliged to devote themselves are too continuous and too positive to allow them to throw themselves into vague abstractions and ambitions.'

The churches

Finally, the churches were important and powerful allies of the kings and princes in Germany. The south of Germany and the Rhineland were predominantly Roman Catholic in religious loyalties. This gave the people of these areas a strong link with Austria. Under Pope Pius IX the Catholic church set its face against the trends of the times – Pius IX believed that liberalism and nationalism were the greatest evils of the age – and Catholics were taught by their priests to respect the authority of kings and princes. In the north and east the main religion was Protestant and here the Lutheran Evangelical church predominated. According to the Lutheran faith kings were ordained by God to maintain order in an evil world. Subjects of the king had no right to resist, even if their ruler was a tyrant. In Prussia the Lutheran church was the official state church and a vital prop of the King's authority.

FORCES FOR CHANGE

With such powerful forces ranged in favour of the status quo it is not surprising that Germany changed so little in the years 1815–48. Some changes, however, did occur due to a number of factors.

Industry

Parts of Germany began to experience an industrial revolution in the 1820s and 1830s. Germany had coal reserves in the area of the River Ruhr, the Saarland and Silesia. There were deposits of iron ore and other minerals.

There were pockets of industrial development all over Germany by the 18th century: cotton was made in Elberfeld and Barmen; steel cutlery at Remscheid and Solingen; Krefeld was known for its silk, Dresden for its pottery. Hamburg and Bremen had developed as ports engaged in the Atlantic trade and Frankfurt had become an important banking centre. Most of these industries still, at the beginning of the 19th century, used traditional handcraft methods of manufacture, but in the 1820s some enterprising industrialists began to introduce new, large machines, based in factories and the steam engines to drive them from Britain. The number of steam engines rose from 400 in 1834 to 1200 in 1850. Most of them were in the manufacturing districts of Prussia and Saxony.

Railways

The building of railways gave industrial development a major boost. The first railway line in Germany, along a 6-kilometre stretch from Nuremberg to Furth, was opened in 1835. By 1846 there were over 2000 kilometres of railway line across Germany. The railways created a new era in industrial expansion and brought far-reaching social changes.

- New jobs were created in building and running the railways.
- New era in heavy industry: the railways needed coal and iron rails, locomotives and rolling stock, most of which were initially brought from Britain, but by 1850 many of the materials needed by the railways were produced in Germany itself.
- Railways also stimulated the growth of towns; in 1815 only fourteen German towns had populations of more than 100,000 inhabitants, by 1850 many more towns in the main industrial areas had large and growing populations.
- Despite the political difficulties of building railways across state borders, a railway network was created which linked together all the main German cities and made travel around the country easier and more common.

All this helped to engender a greater sense of unity among some sections of the population. As one historian has put it: 'In a Germany served by express trains running from Aachen to Berlin and from Hamburg to Munich, the Main gradually ceased to divide the north from the south, while the Elbe no longer separated the east from the west.'

The artisans

Even with these changes, however, Germany could not be described as an industrialised country by 1848. Working in large factories or other large-scale enterprises was not the typical experience of most Germans, even amongst those engaged in manufacture. Most German workers were *Handwerker* (artisans) who continued to employ traditional handicraft methods of manufacture. The position of the Handwerker was being undermined by the introduction of new machinery, which made their skills obsolete, and by the abolition of old laws designed to protect their livelihoods. The result was that they were becoming increasingly discontented and restless in the 1840s, particularly after the economic crisis of 1847 (see page 14) which left many of them unemployed.

Middle class

As trade and industry expanded, so too did the middle class. The merchants, bankers and industrialists who grew in wealth found it increasingly irksome that the landed aristocracy still enjoyed social privileges; for example, in Prussia the front seats at theatres were still reserved for members of the aristocracy. Political divisions in Germany were a serious barrier to the expansion of trade. Separate currencies, different business laws, different systems of weights and measures and internal customs barriers all

Contemporary engraving of a food riot in Stettin, East Prussia, 1847.

frustrated the entrepreneur who wished to expand trade beyond the frontiers of the home state. The governments of these states, being dominated by princes and aristocrats, knew more about agriculture than they did about commerce. Thus when industrialists met together in their local chambers of commerce or at trade fairs and congresses, the discussions inevitably turned to the need for political change. Among the middle class there were also many professional people: doctors, lawyers, university professors and journalists. It was from among this group that the first stirrings of political debate and criticism of the existing system began to emerge, but by 1848 only a minority of the middle class was politically active. There were no political parties, and no political mass movement.

Political ideas

New political ideas of the period can be broadly classified under the headings of **liberalism** and **nationalism**.

- Liberalism was a body of ideas which appealed mainly to the middle class, people of property who believed that their contribution to the economic life of their country should be recognised by giving them the right to vote and to participate in government. Most 19th-century liberals were opposed to full democracy since they believed that giving the vote to peasants and workers would lead to mob rule. In Germany liberalism was a minority creed before 1848 and also a deeply divided one. In the south and west, where French influence was strongest, the movement tended to be more radical in character and many liberals advocated a republican form of government. In the north more moderate liberals wanted to persuade the princes to give up some of their power and they looked for a lead to the King of Prussia.

- Nationalism was also a set of ideas which was growing in popularity across Europe in the first half of the 19th century. German nationalists wished to see the German people united into one nation-state, a new German Reich. They expressed pride in the achievements of German writers, composers and philosophers, and sought to identify a German national spirit which set Germans apart from other nationalities. Some nationalists took this a stage further and emphasised the racial superiority of the German people. There was pride in the German contribution to the defeat of Napoleon in 1813–14, in which the Prussian armies had played a crucial role. Thus many nationalists regarded Prussian military strength and its authoritarian system of government as the true embodiment of the German national spirit. Not all nationalists could agree on the true extent of the German nation-state they wished to create and these divisions would be a serious problem in 1848. During the 1840s nationalism in Germany was given a major boost by an apparent threat by France to invade Germany in 1840 and a dispute with Denmark over the duchies of Schleswig and Holstein in 1846.

THE ROLE OF PRUSSIA

Reformers in Germany increasingly looked to Prussia to give a lead. As the second largest state within the Confederation, and with a large, well-organised and well-led army, Prussia would be the only German state capable of challenging Austria. Moreover, during the 18th century Prussia had expanded its territory in the face of Austrian opposition. In the peace settlement of 1815 Prussia had gained territory in north-western Germany (in the Rhineland and Westphalia). This made Prussia the dominant state in northern Germany and also the guardian of German territory against invasion by France, a highly symbolic status in the eyes of German nationalists. In the years 1807–15 there had been a number of reforms in Prussia under which serfdom was abolished, the army and civil service were modernised and the education system was improved. After 1816, however, **King Friedrich Wilhelm III** stopped the reform process and adopted a policy of co-operation with Austria.

Zollverein

Prussia did take the lead in forging the economic unity of Germany. In 1818 a *Zollverein* (customs union) was established within Prussia's own territories. This created a single system of tariffs for the movement of goods around Prussia. Gradually the Zollverein was extended until by 1834 an all-German customs union had been established under Prussia's leadership. Significantly, Austria was

---

KEY PERSON

Friedrich Wilhelm III. King of Prussia 1797–1840, he led the state during the wars against Napoleon. Under his rule the Prussian army and other aspects of Prussian society were reformed so that Prussia was able to play a vital role in the defeat of France in 1814. He also promised to grant a constitution but, under pressure from Metternich and from reactionary Prussian aristocrats, he abandoned his reform programme.

excluded. The Austrian delegate to the Diet (Assembly) of the Confederation well understood the significance of this when he remarked: 'The Zollverein is one of the chief nails in the coffin of the German Confederation . . . Prussia is now taking over the actual leadership of Germany's policy, Austria's leadership being merely formal.' The Zollverein stimulated the development of trade and industry throughout Germany and also made manufacturers and merchants realise that more rapid progress could be made if other aspects of economic life were brought under unified control.

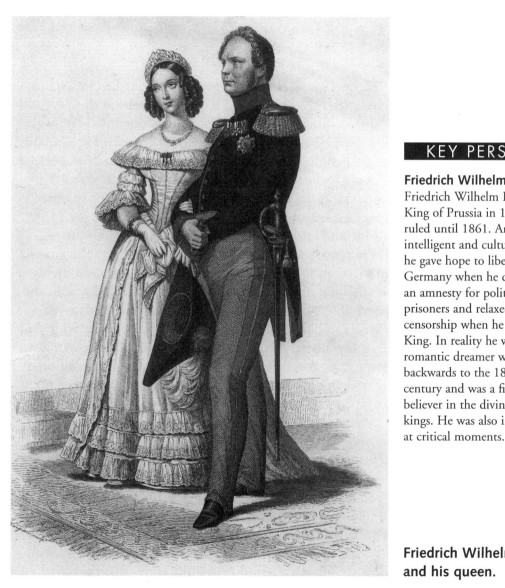

Friedrich Wilhelm IV and his queen.

KEY PERSON

Friedrich Wilhelm IV.
Friedrich Wilhelm IV became King of Prussia in 1840 and ruled until 1861. An intelligent and cultured man, he gave hope to liberals in Germany when he declared an amnesty for political prisoners and relaxed press censorship when he became King. In reality he was a romantic dreamer who looked backwards to the 18th century and was a firm believer in the divine right of kings. He was also indecisive at critical moments.

Friedrich Wilhelm IV. In 1840 a new Prussian King, Friedrich Wilhelm IV, acceded to the throne and reformers believed that he would be more sympathetic to liberal and nationalist ideas than his predecessor. In 1847 he seemed to live up to their expectations when he convened a new assembly, the United Diet. This body, however, was allowed no real power and was not a genuine parliament. Indeed, when Friedrich Wilhelm opened the Diet he made his real intentions abundantly clear. 'Never will I permit', he said, 'a written sheet of paper (a **constitution**) to come between our God in heaven and this land . . . to rule us with its paragraphs and supplant the old sacred loyalty.' Thus, even though Prussia was in many ways a force for change in Germany and the focus of the hopes of many liberal nationalists, any changes which did occur would be under the control and direction of the Prussian monarchy.

KEY FACT

Constitutions. A constitution is a written body of laws which define the powers of the government and the rights of the citizen. In 1848 very few European states had written constitutions.

SUMMARY QUESTIONS

1 What was particularism? Why were the German princes one of the main obstacles to German unity?

2 Why were (a) aristocrats, (b) peasants and (c) the churches supporters of the status quo?

3 How did (a) the railways and (b) the Zollverein contribute to the growing movement for greater unity?

4 Why were the members of the middle class the main supporters of the ideas of liberalism and nationalism?

5 To what extent was Prussia a force for change in Germany?

CHAPTER 2

The 1848 revolutions

START OF THE REVOLUTIONS

In February 1848 the French King, Louis Philippe, was overthrown by a popular uprising in Paris. News of this event spread across Europe and stimulated protests, demonstrations and uprisings against other monarchs. In Germany, still suffering the effects of the **economic crisis** of 1847–8, there were widespread outbreaks of unrest.

- Rhineland – attacks on millowners.
- Thuringia and Saxony – attacks on factory machinery by artisans.
- Baden – a peasant uprising which spread northwards.
- Vienna – a revolution in March which forced the resignation of Metternich.
- Berlin – barricades were erected in the streets and clashes between the army and the demonstrators led to the Prussian King, Friedrich Wilhelm IV, withdrawing his troops from the city. He appointed new liberal ministers and promised to call elections for a new assembly.
- Bavaria – in Munich King Ludwig I was overthrown, mainly due to his personal unpopularity.
- Baden – a group of radicals tried to overthrow the ruler and set up a **republic.** The revolt was crushed by local troops reinforced by detachments from neighbouring states.

Across Germany princes began to dismiss conservative ministers, promised to grant constitutions and summoned elected assemblies. In the main bloodless, the revolution appeared to have been successful, although it was only in Bavaria that the king was overthrown.

The Frankfurt Parliament

Elections. Liberal nationalists all over Germany now saw the chance to create a new, united Germany; at the end of March liberal politicians met at Frankfurt in the so-called *Vorparliament* (preliminary parliament) to make

KEY ISSUES

Universal suffrage. In a truly democratic political system the suffrage (right to vote) would be granted to all adult citizens. This is known as universal suffrage.

Indirect elections. These involved dividing voters into groups, often on a social class basis. Each group would elect representatives, who would then choose the delegate to the Parliament. This system contained a deliberate bias against 'lower-class' voters.

Barricade in Berlijn.

1848 revolutionaries defend their barricade.

arrangements for the setting up of a National Constituent Assembly. 574 representatives met in St Paul's Church in Frankfurt for five days. After a struggle between radical politicians (who wanted **universal suffrage**) and moderates over the franchise for the elections to the National Assembly, a compromise was reached which granted the right to vote to every citizen of majority age who was 'independent'. Only men were allowed to vote and it was left to each individual state to define what constituted independence. Some states interpreted this more widely than others and in most states there were **indirect elections**. When the elections were held, therefore, they resulted in the return of an overwhelmingly middle-class Assembly. Not a single working man was elected and only one peasant; there were few landowners or businessmen and over 200 lawyers with substantial numbers of university professors, teachers and civil servants. Many of these men, however, possessed considerable ability.

Power of the Assembly. Meetings began in May 1848. **Heinrich von Gagern,** a moderate liberal, was elected President of the Assembly, and the brother of the Austrian Emperor, Archduke John, was elected to the position of Imperial Regent (head of state). Ministers were appointed and the Assembly declared that when the national constitution had been drawn up it would take precedence over the constitutions of the individual states. The Assembly thus began to assume the trappings of state power without any of the institutions which could make that power a reality:

- Ministers had no civil service to implement their decisions
- The Assembly had no army of its own
- Real power in Germany still rested in the hands of the individual states.

Such authority as the Assembly possessed was purely moral. Many Germans took pride in the creation of a National Assembly, the first truly national institution in German history, but the majority of Germans also wanted to preserve the identity and independence of their own state.

Schleswig-Holstein affair

This contradiction was clearly exposed during the **Schleswig-Holstein** affair. In March 1848 there was a rebellion by the Germans in the duchies against the Danish King and the rebels appealed to the German Confederation for help. The Federal Diet asked Prussia to intervene on behalf of the Confederation. Prussian troops entered Schleswig–Holstein and drove the Danish forces out, to general acclaim from German nationalists in the Frankfurt Parliament. The Prussian action, however, had aroused opposition from other great powers such as Great Britain, and had not been supported by Austria. Friedrich Wilhelm IV, therefore, ordered his troops to leave Schleswig–Holstein and agreed to an armistice with Denmark. His actions met with opposition in the Frankfurt Parliament as they were seen as a betrayal of German nationalism but the threat of a clash with Prussia,

The position of Schleswig and Holstein.

one of the most powerful German states, persuaded the majority in the Parliament to acquiesce in Prussia's action. The radical minority in the Parliament, however, opposed the armistice and called on their supporters outside Parliament to demonstrate in the streets. The fact that the demonstrations were put down by Austrian and Prussian troops was a serious blow to the Parliament's claim to represent the will of the people. Moreover, the episode revealed fundamental divisions within the Parliament over its future course of action.

Constitution. Throughout 1848–9 the Frankfurt Parliament continued its debates on a new German constitution and the frontiers of the new Germany. By March 1849 the constitution was finished and was ready to be submitted to the individual German states for their approval. The success or failure, therefore, depended on the consent of the rulers of the old Germany, and in particular on the consent of the Austrian Emperor and the King of Prussia. If the revolutions of 1848 had seriously weakened their authority the decisions of the Frankfurt Parliament might have been implemented, but by March 1849 both the Emperor and Friedrich Wilhelm IV had restored their authority in their respective dominions.

Revolution in Austria

In Austria the news from Paris had stimulated political activity among the middle and lower classes. Petitions calling for reform began flooding in to the Emperor and, on 13 March, a demonstration in Vienna resulted in violent clashes with troops. The imperial court was seized with panic. Metternich was forced to resign and the Emperor promised a **new constitution**. He also appointed new ministers. Despite making many concessions to liberal demands it failed to satisfy the most radical elements among the students, factory workers and the Handwerker of Vienna. In May 1848 further demonstrations in Vienna forced the Emperor to promise a parliament elected by universal suffrage.

Counter-revolution in Austria. Emperor Ferdinand fled to the city of Innsbruck where, surrounded by reactionary army officers and aristocratic advisers, he plotted a counter-revolution. The army had already achieved some success in suppressing revolts in the provinces of the Empire. Windischgratz had put down the revolt amongst the Czech people of Prague in June, and Radetsky had achieved success against the revolt in northern Italy in August. Against the nationalist revolt in Hungary, which threatened to separate Hungary from the rest of the Empire, progress in restoring imperial authority was much slower. By the summer of 1848, however, the Emperor was starting to deploy a policy of divide and rule by encouraging the Croat, Serb and Romanian people who lived in Hungary to revolt against their new Hungarian rulers. The result was a civil war in Hungary which was finally ended, and Austrian rule re-established, by the intervention of a Russian army in March 1849.

Revolution crushed. By the autumn of 1848 the revolution in Vienna itself was in crisis. An outbreak of violence in the streets frightened the middle class, who feared for their property if 'mob rule' was allowed to get out of hand. Only the monarchy and the army had the necessary power to restore order. The peasants also saw the monarchy as their best defence against the landowners. When Windischgratz led an army into Vienna and crushed the revolution in November, 2000 Viennese were killed in the fighting, the bloodiest repression seen anywhere in Europe during the events of 1848. With monarchical authority restored, a new ministry under **Schwarzenberg** was appointed. In December, in a move designed to further strengthen the monarchy, Emperor Ferdinand was persuaded by his ministers to abdicate: he was succeeded by his nephew, **Franz Josef.**

Revolution in Prussia

By November 1848 counter-revolution had also triumphed in Prussia. The outlook had seemed very different in March when the revolution began. Inspired by the news from Paris and Vienna, and fuelled by high unemployment caused by the economic crisis of 1847, crowds took to the streets of Berlin and there were violent clashes with the army. In response, Friedrich Wilhelm IV took various steps:

KEY PEOPLE

Schwarzenberg. Prince Felix zu Schwarzenberg was Austrian Chancellor from 1848 to 1852. A soldier and diplomat by training, he was totally committed to maintaining the power of the Austrian Emperor. He was described as haughty and arrogant, cynical and unscrupulous, but he also had great political skill.

Emperor Franz Josef. Franz Josef became Emperor in 1848 at the age of eighteen and ruled until 1916. Described as a moderate and decent man who ruled out of a sense of duty to his people, he had complete faith in his divine right to rule. He was an absolute monarch who was rigid and unimaginative in his thinking but he was nevertheless forced to make compromises with the forces of liberalism and nationalism during his long reign.

- He promised a new constitution, new ministers and that Prussia would take an active role in the creation of a new Germany.
- After further violence the King ordered his soldiers to withdraw from the city, even though they were gaining the upper hand in the exchanges with the rioters.
- The King now left himself at the mercy of the crowd and on 21 March he rode through the streets of Berlin wearing the black, red and gold colours of the revolutionaries.
- After further attempting to appease the crowd with the promise 'Henceforth Prussia is merged in Germany', he appointed a new ministry led by two middle-class liberal politicians, Auerwald and Hansemann.

Prussian National Assembly. This was an assembly elected by universal suffrage. When it met in May it proved to have a radical majority which was in favour of abolishing the tax privileges of the aristocracy. This alarmed the landowners. Further violence in the streets of Berlin in May also alarmed the middle class and the liberal ministers at the head of the new government. The army was recalled to Berlin to maintain order. Thus a ministry which depended for its authority on the popular revolt which had brought it to power was increasingly forced to rely on the King and his army to save it from its own former supporters. For his part Friedrich Wilhelm IV had withdrawn from Berlin with his entourage and taken refuge in Potsdam, where he was surrounded by reactionary advisers who tried to persuade him to reassert his authority. The King has been described as both two-faced and irresolute in the way he dealt with the situation in 1848. From Potsdam he periodically travelled to Berlin to meet his ministers, men from the middle class for whom he had nothing but contempt. In Potsdam he denounced those same ministers. Realising that the King was not prepared to accept any constitutional limitations on his powers, Auerswald and Hansemann resigned in the summer.

Counter-revolution in Prussia. Another outbreak of violence in Berlin in October gave the King an excuse to act. He appointed his uncle, the aristocratic Count

Brandenburg, as his chief minister and increased the strength of the army in Berlin. The Prussian National Assembly was ordered to leave the city and Berlin was placed under martial law. In Berlin itself the counter-revolution was virtually bloodless: the opposition was by this stage too weak to resist. Sporadic outbreaks of violent resistance in Silesia and the Rhineland were crushed by the army. When the Prussian National Assembly tried to re-convene in the town of Brandenburg in December, in defiance of the King, he dissolved the Assembly. On the very same day, however, he granted a constitution of his own free will (see page 25). By the end of 1848 royal authority had been re-established in Prussia as well as Austria and the revolution in Germany was effectively over.

NEW GERMAN CONSTITUTION

While these events were taking place in Vienna and Berlin, the Frankfurt Parliament was just beginning its debates on the new German constitution. The Parliament was seriously divided within itself between the radical left, the liberal centre and the right.

- The left-wing deputies advocated a republican form of government involving the overthrow of the princes and the establishment of a democratic form of government. They formed a substantial minority at Frankfurt.
- On the right was another minority group who defended the rights of the princes and who wished to restrict the role which a national parliament would play in the future Germany.
- The majority, who were moderate liberals, worked for a compromise between the rights of the existing rulers and the rights of the people. They advocated a constitutional monarchy in which power would be shared between princes and parliament and in which the rights of the people would be guaranteed by a written constitution.

These fundamental rights were the subject of the first stage of the debates on the constitution, and an agreed statement of the rights of the people was completed by December. The framing of the constitution took longer because there were more serious disagreements between the various factions and it was not finally ready until March 1849.

Frontiers. Equally difficult to resolve was the issue of defining the frontiers of the new Germany.

- The majority at Frankfurt were satisfied with the proposal that they should include all the states in the existing German Confederation, plus Schleswig and east and west Prussia. This would have the advantage of including the vast majority of the German-speaking peoples of central Europe but it would also include large non-German minorities – the Danes of Schleswig–Holstein, the Czechs of Bohemia and the Poles of east and west Prussia. (See the map on page 4.)
- The Czechs, among whom nationalist feelings were also stirring, objected to their proposed incorporation into a greater Germany and demonstrated this by refusing to participate in the elections for the Frankfurt Parliament.
- In Posen, nationalism was also gaining ground among the Poles who wished to see the restoration of an independent Poland.

Conflict between Polish nationalism and German nationalism came to a head over the issue of Prussia's eastern province of Posen. Mainly Polish in terms of population, Posen contained a large German minority. The King of Prussia initially offered to partition Posen to allow part to join a restored Poland but his proposal involved Prussia keeping the largest share. This proposal was supported by the Frankfurt Parliament, many of whose representatives regarded the Poles as being culturally inferior to the Germans.

KEY CONCEPTS

Kleindeutsch and Grossdeutsch. German nationalists disagreed over the size of the united Germany they were trying to create. The *Kleindeutsch* (little Germany) party advocated a Germany which would exclude Austria. The *Grossdeutsch* (greater Germany) party wanted a Germany that included Austria.

Grossdeutsch or Kleindeutsch? In the spring and summer of 1848 there was an expectation among the representatives at Frankfurt that the Austrian Empire would break up as the eastern half of the Empire would break away and become an independent Hungary. This would leave Austria and Bohemia free to be incorporated into a new, united Germany. When this did not happen the representatives at Frankfurt were faced with a dilemma over the exact relationship between a united Germany and the Austrian Empire. There were two main schools of thought on this issue:

- The *Kleindeutsch* party advocated a Germany from which Austria and Bohemia would be excluded altogether and Prussia would be the predominant power within Germany. This was a proposal which appealed to the Prussians and also to the representatives from the smaller states.

- The *Grossdeutsch* party insisted that Austria and Bohemia, being German lands, must be included in any future united Germany. This was a solution favoured by the larger states and by Catholics.

Indeed at the beginning of the debates on this issue a majority at Frankfurt supported the *Grossdeutsch* solution as being the only genuine expression of German nationalism, but by March 1849 the majority had swung round to supporting the *Kleindeutsch* idea. This was a result of developments within Austria itself.

- The Austrian view. After the appointment of Schwarzenberg as chief minister the Austrian delegates at Frankfurt began to adopt an increasingly hostile approach to both the *Grossdeutsch* and *Kleindeutsch* solutions. As an alternative they put forward the idea of a *Mitteleuropa* (mid-European union) of the whole Austrian Empire with the German Confederation, but one which would be a much looser confederation of independent states and which would be dominated by Austria. It was clear that Austria could not be incorporated into a united Germany; of necessity the delegates at Frankfurt had to settle for the *Kleindeutsch* solution.

The constitution

The constitution was finally agreed in March 1849.

- It proposed a federal union of Germany in which the individual states and their princes would retain some of their powers over local affairs, but foreign policy, defence and transport would be controlled by the central government of a new united Germany.
- This central government would consist of a Kaiser (Emperor) who would have extensive powers over the appointment and dismissal of ministers and over legislation, and a Reichstag (Parliament).
- The Reichstag would be elected by all adult males; it would have two chambers (upper and lower); and it would have the right to vote on all legislation and on the

annual budget. This was a compromise between the rights of the monarch and the rights of Parliament.

• Friedrich Wilhelm IV was elected Kaiser of the new Germany.

END OF THE REVOLUTION IN GERMANY

When a deputation from Frankfurt set off for Berlin in April formally to offer the crown to Friedrich Wilhelm IV they had some reasons for optimism that their offer would be accepted. Twenty of the smaller German states had already given their approval to the constitution and to the new Kaiser but the five largest states, including Prussia, Bavaria and Saxony, had not yet decided. In Prussia itself Friedrich Wilhelm IV had re-established his authority and, although he had granted a constitution for Prussia, he had shown that he was not prepared to have his powers limited by any parliament. He believed in the **divine right of kings**. When the delegates from Frankfurt met Friedrich Wilhelm IV he declined their offer on the grounds that the crown was not theirs to give. He later referred to the offer as the 'crown by the grace of bakers and butchers'. Prussia rejected the constitution drawn up at Frankfurt and was followed by Bavaria, Saxony and Hanover. The constitution was now finished.

The revolution collapses. Austria and Prussia withdrew their delegates from Frankfurt. Those who were left, mainly radical deputies from south Germany, were ejected from Frankfurt by the city government. Across Germany there were sporadic outbreaks of popular protest in the spring of 1849. The King of Saxony was forced to flee from Dresden but was restored to power by Saxon and Prussian soldiers. There was resistance also in the Rhineland and in Baden but here again Prussian soldiers crushed the uprisings. The rump of the Frankfurt Parliament moved to Stuttgart, the capital of Wurttemberg, but they were dispersed by troops loyal to the local ruler.

The revolution of 1848–9 was over. Across Germany the princes still ruled in their own states and German unity

KEY CONCEPT

Divine right of kings. The idea that kings are chosen by God to rule over their subjects.

seemed as far away as ever. Out of the events of these years, however, did come some positive pointers to the future. In key states such as Prussia constitutions had been granted, civil liberties had been extended and the idea of a united Germany had been placed firmly on the agenda.

SUMMARY QUESTIONS

1 What were the issues that divided the parliamentarians at Frankfurt?

2 How was monarchical power restored in (a) Prussia and (b) Austria?

3 Explain the differences between Grossdeutsch and Kleindeutsch. Why did the Frankfurt Parliament eventually come to favour the Kleindeutsch solution?

4 Why was the restoration of monarchical power in Austria and Prussia a fatal blow to the Frankfurt Parliament?

CHAPTER 3

Germany after the 1848 revolutions

PRUSSIAN CONSTITUTION

When Friedrich Wilhelm IV closed down the Prussian Assembly in December he also rejected the idea of a constitution being forced on him by his subjects. On the very same day, however, he granted a constitution of his own free will but a constitution which reflected the views of his conservative advisers and which retained real power in the hands of the King himself. Under the constitution a Parliament consisting of two chambers, an upper house and a *Landtag* (lower house), was established.

- The upper house was to be elected by men over the age of 30 who owned substantial property.
- The Landtag, on the other hand, was to be elected by all adult Prussian males – a franchise that was among the most liberal of any state in Europe at that time.
- Parliament was given the right to participate in the making of new laws and to vote on the budget.
- The key power of the appointment and dismissal of ministers, however, was retained by the King.
- There were other seemingly liberal aspects of the new constitution. It guaranteed the civil rights of ordinary Prussians, allowing them freedom of person, of movement, of religion, of assembly and to join political parties.

The constitution was well received in Prussia and earned Prussia prestige in the rest of Germany. However, from a liberal point of view the constitution had shortcomings.

- The Parliament could debate important issues and might occasionally come into conflict with the King and his ministers but in any such conflict the King was always the ultimate source of authority. In the event of a serious constitutional conflict arising the King could exercise emergency powers which enabled him to rule by decree, suspend civil rights and collect taxes without the consent of Parliament.

- Above all, a constitution which had been granted by the King's favour could be changed by him. In May 1849, for example, universal suffrage for elections to the Landtag was withdrawn and replaced by a three-class **voting system**.

THE ERFURT UNION

League of Three Kings. Although Friedrich Wilhelm IV had rejected the offer of the crown of a united Germany he still hoped to unite Germany under Prussian leadership. In May 1849, following the advice of his minister **Radowitz**, he persuaded the rulers of Saxony and Hanover to join him in a *Dreikonigsbundnis* (League of Three Kings). This was later expanded into a larger German Union after the rulers of seventeen other states were bullied into joining. A congress to draw up a constitution for the Union was to meet at Erfurt in May 1850; hence the enterprise has been named the Erfurt Union. The foundations of this Union, however, were shaky from the beginning. Saxony would only join if Bavaria also became a member; Hanover's participation was conditional on Austria being included in the federal state. The Union was a challenge to Austria's predominance in Germany and, when it was first founded, Austria was still preoccupied with suppressing revolution in Hungary. By August 1849, however, Austria was ready to reassert its authority in Germany.

Schwarzenberg's first move was to negotiate a temporary agreement with Prussia whereby the two states agreed to administer Germany jointly until May 1850. This weakened Prussia's prestige in the eyes of the smaller states which began to break away from the Erfurt Union. Bavaria and Wurttemberg decided not to join, which provided Saxony and Hanover with the excuse to secede. In May 1850, when the temporary agreement lapsed, Shwarzenberg decided to revive the old German Confederation and its Federal Diet at Frankfurt under the presidency of Austria. All states were invited to send

KEY SYSTEM

The Prussian voting system. Deputies to the Prussian Landtag were not elected directly. The voters in each constituency were divided into three classes according to the amount of tax they paid. Each class chose representatives who, in turn, selected the deputies. This system gave a disproportionate influence to the upper and middle classes.

KEY PERSON

Radowitz. Joseph von Radowitz was a Catholic aristocrat who had served as a general in the Prussian army. Gifted and energetic, he was a close friend of the King and was given control over the foreign ministry in 1849. He had some sympathy with German nationalism and was one of the originators of the idea of the Erfurt Union but his loyalties were firmly on the side of the Prussian monarchy.

representatives to discuss a new constitution and a new central authority for Germany. Prussia refused to attend and a confrontation between Austria and Prussia over the leadership of Germany seemed inevitable.

Humiliation of Olmutz

It was a crisis in the small state of **Hesse-Cassel** which brought matters to a head. Faced with mounting opposition from his subjects and the collapse of his authority, the Elector fled to Frankfurt and appealed to the Federal Diet for assistance. Austria, Bavaria and Wurttemberg signed an alliance and the Diet authorised an Austrian army to march northwards into Hesse-Cassel. This was a serious challenge to Prussia. At this critical moment Friedrich Wilhelm IV again wavered. Radowitz urged him to prepare for war, but he was warned by Russia that it was prepared to support Austria in any conflict. Friedrich Wilhelm IV backed down, but not without one last defiant gesture involving a small skirmish between Austrian and Prussian troops in Hesse-Cassel. Radowitz resigned and the King accepted an Austrian ultimatum that Prussia should accept the occupation of Hesse-Cassel. In an agreement signed at Olmutz in November Prussia agreed to abandon the Erfurt Union and accepted the restoration of the Confederation.

This was the most serious crisis in relations between Austria and Prussia in 60 years. It was a serious defeat for Prussia, made worse by the fact that it was due almost entirely to the King's indecisiveness. Austria's power in Germany was restored but the situation in Germany was now very different from the pre-1848 years. Co-operation between Austria and Prussia was now dead, replaced by a serious rivalry which had the potential to lead to war.

Political reaction

Politically, the 1850s in Germany was a period of reaction as the princes endeavoured to revive their powers.
- In Austria the 1849 constitution was suspended.
- The Federal Diet declared the 'Fundamental Rights of the German People', one of the few remaining legacies of the Frankfurt Parliament, null and void.
- In Prussia press censorship was restored, schools were placed under church control and the aristocracy

re-established their privileged positions in the army and the civil service.

It was not possible, however, to restore the status quo which had existed before 1848, nor did the majority of princes regard this as a desirable policy. In an effort to consolidate peasant support for conservative regimes, feudal obligations which peasants owed to landlords were gradually dismantled. In Prussia, for example, 640,000 peasants concluded their feudal obligations with loans from government-sponsored banks, between 1850 and 1865. Despite the determination of the princes to hold on to their powers there was also a realisation that absolutism had to make some accommodation with the demands for constitutional rule. The Elector of Hesse-Cassel, on the other hand, stubbornly refused any concessions to his subjects and refused to grant a constitution, in the face of mounting opposition. In 1862 Prussia and Austria forced the Elector to grant a constitution.

ECONOMIC CHANGE

It was in the economic field that Germany experienced the most significant changes in the 1850s and 1860s. Building on the foundations laid in the pre-1848 period, the German economy made rapid progress in the post-revolutionary years. Indeed this was the period when, in the view of economic historians, the German economy achieved **take-off** into sustained economic growth and industrialisation. It was also the period when Germany became continental Europe's largest producer of key industrial commodities such as coal and iron, overtaking France and Belgium's combined output of these products by 1871. There was expansion in all sectors of industry. New mines and ironworks were opened in the Ruhr valley, new railways built, steel mills employing the latest steel-making processes were established, and the production of textiles, chemicals and electrical equipment all increased. In the words of Max Wirth, 'tall chimneys grew like mushrooms' in the Ruhr. This was also the period when the names of leading German industrialists like the **Krupps**

KEY STATISTICS

German coal production

1846	3.2m tons
1860	12.3m tons
1871	29.4m tons

KEY COMPANIES

The **Krupp** company of Essen was founded by Alfred Krupp, an entrepreneur and pioneer in the field of iron and steel production. Through its success in producing high-quality steel the company expanded into the production of weapons for the Prussian army.

The **Siemens** company was founded by Werner Siemens, the inventor of the dynamo. It grew into one of the largest and most successful electrical engineering companies in the world by the end of the 19th century.

The **Borsig** company of Berlin produced steam engines and railway locomotives. At a time when British manufacturers were the main suppliers of locomotives, Borsig built a reputation for the high quality of its products and became the main supplier to German railways.

of Essen, **Borsig** of Berlin and **Siemens** became known outside Germany as world leaders in their respective fields.

Prussian economic power. Much of this industrial expansion took place within Prussia. The Ruhr, Silesia and the Saarland were all within Prussian territory. In the 1860s about two-thirds of Germany's ironworks lay in Prussian territory. The balance of economic power within Germany, therefore, was shifting heavily in favour of Prussia. The Prussian government and its army chiefs were well aware of the strategic implications of these developments. The army had an influence on the building of new railway lines since these would in the future be important in the movement of troops. When Alfred Krupp exhibited his six-pounder field gun with a cast steel barrel at the Crystal Palace in 1851 he signalled the start of a major armaments industry in Prussia which would be a decisive factor in future wars.

RELATIONS BETWEEN AUSTRIA AND PRUSSIA

Relations between Austria and Prussia continued to be strained after the events of 1849–50. International conflicts were a feature of the 1850s and Austria and Prussia, as great powers, had to consider their own positions in relation to these conflicts. In 1854 Great Britain, France

The Ruhr valley in West Prussia.

The Krupp works in Essen, 1865.

and Turkey went to war with Russia, a war that became known as the **Crimean war**. Austria, suspicious of Russian intentions in the Balkans, wished to intervene in the war and appealed to the Diet of the German Confederation for support. Friedrich Wilhelm IV was torn between his desire to maintain Prussia's alliance with Austria and his belief that war with Russia was to be avoided. When the Austrian representative to the Diet asked for the mobilisation of half of the federal army, his request was vigorously opposed by the Prussian representative, **Otto von Bismarck**. Bismarck argued that the war did not affect Germany's vital interests. The other states agreed and, for the first time, Austria was outmanoeuvred and isolated in the Confederation.

Zollverein. Austria was again outmanoeuvred over its plan to link the Zollverein with an Austrian customs union, thereby creating a mid-European customs union which would open up trade throughout central Europe and stimulate Austria's economy. The plan was opposed by Prussia since it would pose a threat to Prussia's economic dominance in northern and central Germany. Pressure was put on the smaller German states and the Zollverein treaty was renewed by all the states on Prussia's terms.

War in Italy. In 1859 Austria was involved in a war against France and the Kingdom of Sardinia over its territories in northern Italy. The threat of French expansionism was a factor that was guaranteed to arouse German national feeling and there was also much sympathy in Germany for Austria, a fellow German state. Friedrich Wilhelm IV offered Austria military support but only on condition that Prussia should command the federal forces in the event of a French attack on the Rhineland. Austria refused, unwilling to recognise Prussia's dominance in northern Germany. When Austria was defeated, however, Prussia was blamed for its failure to help an ally. Austria's defeat by Sardinia and France caused her to lose prestige and precipitated a serious financial crisis.

The Crimean war. In 1854 Britain and France went to war in the Near East with the aim of protecting Turkey from Russian aggression. The Allies landed on the Crimean peninsular in the Black Sea, and eventually, in September 1855, captured the Russian port of Sebastopol. The Crimean war had a significant impact on the balance of power in Europe. Austria's failure to support Russia in this war, coming so soon after Russia had intervened to prop up Austrian rule in Hungary in 1849, shattered the long-standing conservative alliance between the two powers. This created a more fluid diplomatic situation in which other powers had more room for manoeuvre.

Location of the Crimean Peninsula.

NATIONALVEREIN

Otto von Bismarck. Born into a *Junker* family in 1815, Bismarck was a staunch defender of the aristocracy but not typical of his class. Well-educated, he was an accomplished linguist and displayed a razor-sharp mind throughout his political career. He was physically strong, restless and ambitious. He had a self-confidence bordering on arrogance, was ruthless and determined in the pursuit of his objectives and he could be vindictive and intolerant towards any opposition.

He first made an impact in 1849–50 when, as a member of the Prussian Parliament, he was an outspoken opponent of the liberals and nationalists. He served as Prussian representative at the Federal Diet 1851–8, Ambassador to Russia 1858–62 and Ambassador to France in 1862.

Rudolf von Bennigsen. Bennigsen came from Hanover. He was the first president of the *Nationalverein* and one of the founders of the National Liberal party in 1866.

The stimulus to national feeling arising out of the war crisis of 1859 was reflected in the formation of a new organisation, the *Nationalverein*. In August leading liberals from all over Germany met at Eisenach and appealed for the formation of a party committed to German unification. In September the Nationalverein was set up with the Hanoverian liberal leader, **Bennigsen**, as its president. This was the first national political organisation in German history. Although its membership was restricted to the middle class by its policy of charging high membership fees, it was able to exert considerable influence through its links with other organisations and through its members among state officials. The Nationalverein attracted support also from leading German industrialists such as Siemens and Meier. *Kleindeutsch* in outlook, the Nationalverein looked to Prussia for leadership in the struggle for German unification. Politically the organisation was liberal but German national liberalism had changed greatly since 1848. No longer were the German liberals romantic idealists. The new generation tended to be more realistic in their attitude to the princes, more aware of the realities of political power. As the leading liberal Frobel wrote in 1859, 'The German nation is sick of principles and doctrines, literary existence and theoretical greatness. What it wants is power, power, power and whoever gives it power, to him it will give honour, more honour than he can imagine.'

THE CONSTITUTIONAL CRISIS OF 1862

Prussian army reforms

In 1862 a serious conflict between the Prussian Parliament and the monarchy led to far-reaching consequences for the future direction of Prussia, and of Germany. The roots of this conflict lay in the need to reform and strengthen the Prussian army, a need which had been first identified in 1859 at the time of the war in Italy between France and Austria. When the Prussian army had been mobilised during this crisis, serious defects had been revealed in Prussia's defences. The new King **Wilhelm I** had appointed **von Roon** as Minister of War to make major reforms in the army; von Roon had proposed a major increase in its size. Prussia had a tradition of compulsory military service for, in theory, all young men. In practice the army's annual intake of 40,000 new recruits had remained static since the 1820s, despite the fact that Prussia's population had nearly doubled during the same period. This discrepancy meant that each year approximately 25,000 young men escaped military service. Those who did join the army spent three years in a front-line regiment, two years in the reserve and fourteen years in the **Landwehr**. By the end of their period in the Landwehr they would be too old for front-line service.

von Roon's reform plans:

- Increase the army's annual intake of recruits to 63,000
- Create 39 new infantry regiments and 10 new cavalry regiments
- Service would in future be three years in a front-line regiment, four years in the reserve and eleven years in the Landwehr.

A Bill containing these proposals was put before the Prussian Parliament in 1860 but ran into opposition from the liberals. Support for the army and its traditions was strong at all levels in Prussian society and the liberals accepted the need to strengthen the army if Prussia was to continue to play a leading role in Germany. The opposition focused on the cost of these reforms and on the reduction in the role of the Landwehr, which was seen as more of a people's army than the regular army. The liberals therefore opposed the changes to the Landwehr and proposed a two-year period of service in the front-line regiments as a means of saving money.

Political conflict

The Prussian constitution allowed the Parliament to debate reform proposals and also to vote on the budget, but left the ultimate authority to introduce reforms with the King and his ministers. Von Roon therefore went ahead and introduced the reforms without Parliament's approval. At this point the liberal opposition in Parliament split. The more radical members broke away from the main body to

Wilhelm I. A soldier by training and by temperament, Wilhelm I was a religious and deeply conservative king. He became regent in 1858 when his father was incapacitated by illness and from the start of his reign he was anxious to avenge the humiliation which Prussia had suffered at the hands of Austria in the Olmutz Declaration. He believed in the traditional Prussian virtues of strong government and military power.

Albrecht von Roon. von Roon became Minister of War under Wilhelm I in 1859. Although conservative in his attitude to the power of the monarchy and the army, he was a reforming minister who aimed to improve the efficiency of the army.

Albrecht von Roon.

KEY INSTITUTION

The Landwehr. The Landwehr was a part-time militia, consisting of older men who had completed their service in the regular army. It had been formed during the war against Napoleon in 1813 and represented the nearest equivalent in Prussian terms to a 'people's army'. It was led by mainly middle-class officers. Although von Roon and the King were concerned at the Landwehr's inefficiency, their main objection to it was that it was a branch of the military that was not totally under the control of the King.

Otto von Bismarck, 1863.

form a new party, the Progressive party; and at the elections in December 1861 the Progressives became the largest single party in the lower house.

The Progressives. The party was not opposed to the reforms in principle but saw this crisis as an opportunity to force the King to grant constitutional reforms which would make Parliament more powerful. They used obstructive tactics in Parliament, refusing to vote for the increased expenditure needed for the army reorganisation. To the King, this was a clear challenge to his authority.

- As Commander-in-Chief of the Prussian army, he would not allow any parliamentary interference in military matters.
- As King, he would not allow himself to be dictated to by Parliament.
- Under the constitution which his father had granted, however, taxation and expenditure required parliamentary approval. He considered abdication.

His closest advisers urged him to suspend the constitution and introduce personal rule. Finally, in September 1862 he was advised by von Roon to recall Otto von Bismarck, a man with a reputation for outspoken views and strong tactics, from his post as Ambassador in Paris and appoint him Minister-President of Prussia.

Bismarck. Bismarck initially approached his task of resolving the crisis with caution. He offered the Progressives a compromise under which he would agree to a two-year period of service in the front line, but the Progressives again refused to pass the budget. Bismarck decided to ignore parliamentary opposition:

- He collected taxes without parliamentary approval, and for the next four years Bismarck collected taxes illegally.
- He introduced the army reforms.
- He curtailed the freedom of the press to stifle criticism
- He put pressure on state officials to ensure their continued loyalty.

Despite their efforts to organise a tax boycott, the Progressives were powerless in the face of this determined assault. Lacking popular support and with a weak and timid leadership they were no match for Bismarck and his **Realpolitik**.

SUMMARY QUESTIONS

1 How liberal was the 1849 Prussian constitution?

2 What was the significance of the Erfurt Union and the Declaration of Olmutz?

3 What was the significance of the Nationalverein?

4 What issues were at stake in the conflict between the King of Prussia and the liberals over army reform?

5 Why did von Roon think Bismarck would be the best choice for Minister-President during the 1862 constitutional crisis?

CHAPTER 4

The unification of Germany, 1862–70

BISMARCK'S AIMS

Since first becoming Prussian representative at the Federal Diet in Frankfurt in 1851 Bismarck had been advising the government to take every opportunity to seize the leadership of Germany. He had played a major role in advising the Prussian government to block Austria's plan for an enlarged Zollverein. In his view a conflict between Austria and Prussia over leadership in Germany would be inevitable, although this conflict need not result in war. For Bismarck, politics was nothing more than a naked struggle for power and the only possible course of action for a great state such as Prussia was the ruthless pursuit of its own self-interest.

KEY QUOTE

'Prussia must build up and preserve her strength for the favourable moment, which has already come and gone many times. Her borders under the treaties of Vienna are not favourable for the healthy existence of the state. The great questions of the day will not be settled by speeches and majority decisions – that was the great mistake of 1848 and 1849 – but by blood and iron.' Bismarck speaking in 1862.

Prussian expansion. In seeking to enlarge Prussia and displace Austria as the leading power in Germany, Bismarck was not pursuing German nationalist aims. He did not set out in 1862 with the intention of uniting Germany. He had contempt for nationalism and liberalism; although he did see himself as a German he was always, first and foremost, a loyal servant of the King of Prussia. A skilled and experienced diplomat he was determined to seize any opportunities that occurred to make Prussia the dominant power in Germany, but he was also acutely aware of the international ramifications of attempting a major change in the balance of power in central Europe. Austrian opposition was guaranteed. Other powers, particularly France and Russia, would be affected by Prussian expansion and might prove an obstacle. Great Britain, although not a continental power, wished to maintain the balance of power in Europe. Whatever Bismarck did within Germany, he needed to pay careful attention to the international situation in order to avoid a hostile coalition of powers being formed against Prussia.

The international situation. In the early 1860s this was unusually favourable for Bismarck's aims. Austrian power was open to question after its defeat in Italy. Austria's relations with Russia were at a low ebb after the Crimean war and Russia was unlikely to intervene in Germany to support Austria, unlike the situation in 1849–50. Finally, both France and Russia were, for their different reasons, seeking to overturn the balance of power in Europe; this would create a more fluid diplomatic situation which Bismarck might be able to exploit.

Polish revolt

Bismarck's first involvement in foreign policy was not a success. In 1863 there was a revolt in the Russian part of **Poland** which the Russian army proceeded to crush with severity. Ignoring the protests of the German liberals, among whom there was considerable sympathy for the cause of Polish nationalism, he sent extra troops into the Prussian part of Poland and sealed off the border with Russian Poland. He also offered the Russians military co-operation in dealing with the revolt. The offer was not gratefully received by the Russian government who did not want any help in Poland and it aroused the antagonism of the other powers. However, French criticism of Russia over its handling of the Polish revolt caused a rift between the two powers which made future co-operation unlikely.

Relations with Austria

Relations with Austria were already strained when Bismarck came to power; when Austria attempted to reform the German Confederation in 1863, Bismarck's opposition caused an even deeper rift. In August 1863 the Austrian Emperor summoned all the German princes to a special congress at Frankfurt to discuss a plan to reform the Confederation. The plan, which would have established regular congresses of the princes, an executive body and a representative assembly, was Austria's attempt to seize the initiative and persuade the princes into a loose form of German unity. Wilhelm I was tempted to attend but Bismarck saw in this scheme serious dangers for Prussia's position. In the reformed Confederation, Austria's dominance of Germany would be perpetuated and Prussia could always be outvoted. Using all his powers of

Poland. The Kingdom of Poland had been partitioned between Russia, Prussia and Austria at the end of the 18th century. Polish nationalists aimed at the independence and reunification of their country.

persuasion, including the threat to resign if the King would not support him, Bismarck forced the King to refuse to attend the congress. Although the congress went ahead and the princes endorsed the Austrian plan the scheme was unworkable without Prussia's participation. Austria's reform plan was killed off.

THE SCHLESWIG–HOLSTEIN CRISIS

A revival of the conflict between German and Danish nationalism over Schleswig–Holstein gave Bismarck his next opportunity to enlarge Prussia, although at the start of the crisis this had not seemed to be a likely outcome. Following the earlier conflict between the German Confederation and Denmark in 1848 the status of the duchies had been clarified by the **Treaty of London** in 1852, a treaty which was signed by all the great powers, including Austria and Prussia.

Danish aggression. Over the next ten years relations between Germans and Danes deteriorated and the rights of Germans within the duchies continued to be a cause which ignited strong nationalist sentiments throughout Germany. In 1863 the crisis began when the Danish King, Frederick VII, attempted to incorporate Schleswig into Denmark. This caused an outburst of nationalist feeling in Germany. The German Duke Frederick of Augustenberg proclaimed himself Duke of Schleswig–Holstein and the Confederation began consideration of a plan to incorporate an independent Schleswig–Holstein into the German Confederation. Volunteers across Germany enlisted for a war to free the duchies from Danish control and many of the German princes, swept along by the tide of popular feeling, recognised Frederick of Augustenberg as the legitimate ruler of the duchies.

Bismarck's policy
Prussian annexation? Bismarck was unmoved by this upsurge of popular nationalism. For him, the preferred outcome would be Prussian annexation of the duchies; he did not want to see the creation of another independent state in northern Germany. Prussian annexation, however,

KEY EVENT

Treaty of London. Under this treaty the Danish King had been confirmed as the sovereign power over the duchies but he had also guaranteed that Schleswig would never be fully incorporated into Denmark, that the two duchies would have their own local constitutions and that Germans and Danes would enjoy equal rights within the territories.

would be opposed by Austria, by the other powers which had signed the London Treaty and by German nationalists.

Alliance with Austria. Bismarck's other preferred option, therefore, was for the duchies to remain under Danish control. During the early months of the crisis, Bismarck adopted a cautious, conservative approach which was strictly in line with Prussia's obligations under the Treaty of London. Austria, which would also view the triumph of German nationalism in Schleswig–Holstein as a threat, was on the defensive in this crisis and prepared to work with Prussia to prevent the Confederation from recognising the Duke of Augustenberg and intervening in the duchies. In December 1863 this threat came a step nearer to being a reality when Confederation forces entered Holstein. In January 1864, therefore, Austria entered into an alliance with Prussia to take joint action over the duchies; two weeks later their forces crossed the frontier into Schleswig.

War against Denmark. The war was short, but when Denmark was defeated at Duppel it was clear that the status of the duchies would have to change. A conference was held in London to resolve the issue but the refusal of the Danish King to compromise over the status of Schleswig lost him international support. This also freed Prussia from its obligations under the Treaty of London and allowed Bismarck to manipulate the situation to Prussia's advantage. The war flared up again briefly in the summer of 1864 and resulted in a decisive defeat for Denmark. The fate of the duchies was now in the hands of the victorious powers, Austria and Prussia.

CONFLICT BETWEEN AUSTRIA AND PRUSSIA

Agreement between the two powers, however, proved difficult to achieve. Bismarck's ultimate aim was Prussian annexation of the duchies, an outcome which Austria would be bound to resist. Austria's only other alternative, now that Danish sovereignty had been destroyed, would be to recognise Schleswig–Holstein as an independent state under the Duke of Augustenberg. When Austria proposed this Bismarck, anxious to avoid a conflict with Austria at this stage, was forced to agree but he made his agreement conditional on the Duke of Augustenberg accepting that the duchies would be subject to strict Prussian supervision. This proposal was rejected, as Bismarck had intended that it should be, and the long-term future of the duchies was left unresolved. In the short term, Austria and Prussia agreed on a joint control over the two duchies, a solution that was bound to lead to future conflict between the two powers over the administration of the duchies.

Bismarck's basic aims of annexing the two duchies and establishing Prussian dominance in northern Germany were not forgotten in the diplomatic manoeuvrings and wranglings of the next two years. Although the dispute over Schleswig–Holstein did eventually lead to war between Austria and Prussia in 1866, Bismarck did not set out with the intention of provoking Austria into war. Indeed, with Austria virtually bankrupt and still struggling with the effects of military defeat in Italy in 1859, Bismarck believed there was a good chance that Austria might concede the duchies to Prussia peacefully. Rather late in the day, however, there was a growing realisation in the Austrian government that they had been outmanoeuvred by Bismarck and, under a new ministry led by Mensdorff and Esterhazy, a determination to resist Prussia's expansion.

Convention of Gastein. The Austrian government, in the spring of 1865, came out in favour of recognising the Duke of Augustenberg as the legitimate ruler of Schleswig–Holstein. This was the solution which was favoured by many other German states and by German nationalists. When a proposal to this effect was debated in the Confederation Diet in April 1865, Austria and Prussia were on opposing sides. The motion was defeated. Relations between Austria and Prussia deteriorated during the summer of 1865 but a compromise agreement was reached between the Austrian Emperor, Franz Josef, and King Wilhelm I of Prussia, meeting at Bad Gastein in August. The Convention of Gastein laid down that Austria would administer Holstein and Prussia administer Schleswig, although both powers would have joint sovereignty over the two duchies.

Diplomatic manoeuvres. Bismarck viewed this agreement as a temporary measure, describing it as a 'stopping up of the cracks in the building'. He was still determined to force Austria out of Holstein and, since this carried the risk of war, he had to take care that other powers would not intervene on Austria's side. The main potential threat in this respect came from France. In October 1865 Bismarck visited the French Emperor, **Napoleon III**, at Biarritz and discussed the French position in the event of war. Napoleon was encouraged by Bismarck to remain neutral in an Austro-Prussian conflict with hints that France might gain territory in the Rhineland and by the suggestion that Austria's remaining Italian territory in Venetia would be given to Italy. Napoleon III expected the war to be long and costly and that he would be able to step in and impose his own peace terms on the two exhausted powers.

Alliance with Italy. With French neutrality assured, Bismarck had to take stock of the position of the other powers. Great Britain was clearly unwilling to intervene, as was Russia. In April 1866 Bismarck entered into an alliance with the new and emerging power of Italy which committed Italy to fighting against Austria within three months, thereby facing Austria with the problem of a war on two fronts. With relations between Austria and Prussia deteriorating, both powers began making military preparations for war. Austria then offered to halt its mobilisation if Prussia would do the same and, under pressure from the King, Bismarck agreed. Troop movements in Italy, however, then provoked the Austrians into mobilising their southern army. In response, Prussia began mobilising its armies, an essential first step towards declaring war.

Austro-Prussian war

The final pretext for war was provided by Austria asking the Federal Diet to decide the future of the duchies. This was a **breach of the Gastein Convention** and Prussia announced that it would no longer be bound by it. Bismarck ordered Prussian troops to move into Holstein in a direct challenge to Austria. Austrian forces did not resist immediately. Instead, the Austrian government asked the Confederation for support by mobilising the federal army against Prussia. Bismarck warned the other German states that a vote for this motion would be taken as a declaration of war on Prussia. On 14 June, the motion was carried by nine votes to six in the Diet; only the Thuringian states, Oldenburg, Mecklenburg and the cities of Hamburg, Bremen and Lubeck supporting Prussia. On 15 June Prussia ordered the smaller German states to demobilise and, when this did not happen, Prussian forces occupied Saxony, Hanover and Hesse-Cassel on 16 June. The war had begun.

Defeat of Austria. Contrary to expectations, the war lasted only seven weeks and resulted in a decisive victory for Prussia. Austria was hampered by fighting a war on two fronts, although Italian forces were defeated on land and at sea. Most of the German states were on Austria's side but, due to the meticulous planning by **von Moltke** and to Prussia's superior weaponry, Austrian forces were defeated in the decisive battle at Koniggratz (near the town of Sadowa) in July, after which resistance in south Germany quickly crumbled. Napoleon III stepped in to act as mediator and an armistice was agreed, despite the fact that the Prussian King and his generals were determined to push on with the war and occupy Vienna. Bismarck, however, realised that the longer the war continued the more likely it became that France would intervene. In any event Prussia was in a position to dictate terms and the final Peace of Prague which was signed in August 1866 achieved almost all of Bismarck's immediate objectives.

Peace of Prague. Under the terms of the peace treaty:
- The German Confederation was abolished and replaced by a new North German Confederation from which Austria was excluded.
- This North German Confederation would be dominated by Prussia.
- Schleswig–Holstein, Hanover, Hesse-Cassel, Frankfurt and Nassau were all annexed by Prussia.
- Italy gained Venetia.
- Bavaria, Baden, Wurttemberg and Hesse-Darmstadt all remained independent and Napoleon III insisted that Prussia should respect this.

KEY PERSON

Count von Moltke. A general in the Prussian army, von Moltke became Chief of the General Staff in 1858. He was regarded as a brilliant military strategist.

RESULTS OF THE AUSTRO-PRUSSIAN WAR

Political changes

The changes which the war brought to Germany were so far-reaching and profound that they have been described as the 'revolution of 1866'. In the immediate aftermath of the victory the political landscape in northern Germany was transformed.

Bismarck and the liberals. Since 1862 Bismarck had been locked in a struggle with the liberal opposition in Prussia over his illegal collection of taxes. Bismarck's success in 1866 faced the liberals with a serious dilemma.

- Bismarck, the arch-enemy of liberalism, had succeeded in uniting a large part of Germany, a long-standing liberal ambition.
- Bismarck's success was greeted by a wave of popular support across Germany; in the elections for the Prussian Landtag held after the war there were significant gains for the conservatives at the expense of the liberals.
- Bismarck seized this opportunity to introduce an Indemnity Bill into the Parliament which would give him retrospective approval for his illegal collection of taxes since 1862. The Bill was carried by a large majority.
- The liberals had not only suffered a serious defeat but were also split over their attitude to the Bill. The Progressives opposed the measure whereas more moderate liberals voted in favour. These moderate liberals subsequently joined with liberals in other parts of Germany to form the National Liberal party.

This new party, drawing on support from middle-class business people who had an economic stake in the new Germany, were prepared to compromise with Bismarck and the monarchy and looked to Bismarck to complete the process of unification which he had begun. They would prove to be useful allies for Bismarck in his task of consolidating the unity of the North German Confederation because they were a national party. They also became the largest party in the new Reichstag in the elections of 1867.

Conservative differences. The conservatives in Prussian politics also split and reformed as a result of the events of 1866. Many of the more reactionary elements wanted to exploit the prestige gained for the monarchy to dispense with parliaments and constitutions and revert to a more absolutist style of rule. Bismarck resisted this pressure and his willingness to compromise with liberalism forced a split within the ranks of the conservatives. More reactionary conservatives left the main body to form the Free Conservative party.

North German Confederation

In 1867 the constitution of the North German Confederation was drawn up, reflecting a compromise between the absolute powers of the monarchy and the pressure for constitutional, parliamentary government.

- The King of Prussia was to be the President of the Confederation and he was given exclusive power over foreign policy, the army, declarations of war and the making of peace.
- Ministers were to be appointed by the King and were responsible to him.
- In the other north German states which had not been annexed by Prussia the princes kept their thrones and were allowed to manage their own internal affairs.
- The constitution provided for the creation of new, national institutions. The first of these was the **Bundesrat** (Federal Council) which was a body controlled by the princes and effectively by Prussia.
- There was also to be a Reichstag (National Parliament) which would be elected by universal suffrage. The voting qualification appeared to be a radical concession to the advocates of democracy; in practice, Bismarck believed, the majority of the German population being peasants, universal suffrage would result in conservative majorities in the Reichstag. In any event Bismarck was careful to limit the powers of the Reichstag in a number of ways.
- Any legislation passed by the Reichstag had to be approved by the Bundesrat, giving the princes a veto.
- The Reichstag's control over finance was severely limited. Although there was to be an annual vote on the budget, the only federal taxes which could be collected

KEY TERM

Bundesrat. Each state had a number of representatives on the Bundesrat who were nominated by the princes and who voted according to their instructions. Prussian control of this body was assured by the fact that Prussia had seventeen out of the forty-three representatives and the rule that any constitutional changes would have to be passed by a two-thirds majority, thereby giving Prussia an effective veto.

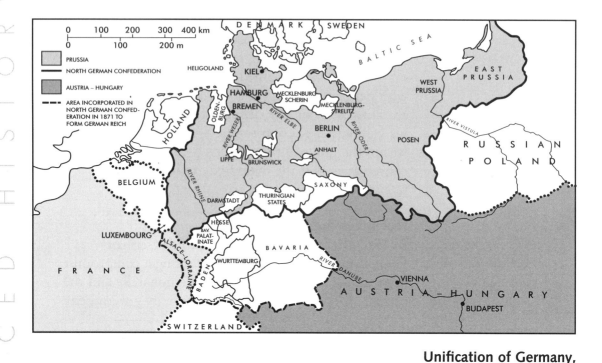

Unification of Germany, 1867–71.

were indirect ones; once these taxes had been agreed their continued collection tended to be automatic.

- Moreover, by far the largest item of government expenditure was on the military and the '**Iron Budget**' was placed outside effective parliamentary control.

Bismarck's own position was pivotal within the new North German Confederation. He remained Minister-President of Prussia and also took on the new role of Chancellor of the Confederation. He also retained responsibility for foreign affairs. Over the next three years, as Bismarck completed the process of German unification, relations with foreign powers and France in particular increasingly occupied centre stage in Germany's affairs.

RELATIONS WITH FRANCE

Napoleon III, who had initially adopted a benign attitude towards German unification, began to be alarmed at the decisive shift in the balance of power that occurred as a result of Prussia's victory in the war of 1866. Subject to domestic political pressures himself and feeling isolated from events, Napoleon III began to seek additional

KEY TERM

The 'Iron Budget'. This was the name given to the separate budget for military expenditure.

territory for France as a means of restoring the balance. In August 1866, therefore, he demanded that France receive territory on the west bank of the Rhine, in the Saarland and the Bavarian Palatinate. Bismarck was able to use Napoleon's demands to pressurise the south German states into signing secret military alliances with the North German Confederation. Under the terms of these alliances the south German states agreed to reform their armies along Prussian lines and to come to the aid of Prussia if she was attacked. Effectively, the south German states started military integration with the north before political unification was achieved. Napoleon III was forced to withdraw his demands in the face of widespread opposition across Germany and relations between France and Prussia had entered a phase of tension and suspicion.

The Luxembourg affair. Napoleon III next turned his attention to Luxembourg, a small duchy on the eastern frontier of France where the population was mainly German-speaking. Luxembourg came under the sovereignty of the King of Holland, had been a member of the German Confederation since 1815 and had a Prussian garrison based on its territory. In 1866, when Bismarck needed Napoleon III's support for Prussia's expansion in Germany, he had hinted that he would not stand in the way of a French annexation of Luxembourg. By 1867 Napoleon III had gained the consent of the Dutch King to sell Luxembourg to France. When news of his intentions became known in Germany there was a national outcry against the plan and the National Liberals demanded that Prussia should defend Germany's honour by resisting a French takeover. Bismarck did not want war with France at this stage but the popular reaction in Germany gave him very little room for compromise. In fact, Bismarck was able to turn the situation to his advantage because the threat of war with France engendered an atmosphere of national crisis at a time when Bismarck was involved in a tense political struggle with the National Liberals over the new constitution. Bismarck was able to play on the patriotism of the Reichstag deputies to persuade them to pass his proposals on the military budget.

Bismarck put pressure on France by revealing the existence of the secret military alliances between Prussia and the south German states. Napoleon III could not find any support for France among other European powers and, when Bismarck suggested a conference of the powers to resolve the issue, Napoleon readily agreed. The subsequent London Conference in 1867 resulted in Luxembourg's independence being guaranteed by all the powers and also in the withdrawal of Prussian forces from the duchy.

French isolation. This was a turning point in relations between Prussia and France. War between them was not yet inevitable but it was becoming a real possibility. At some stage in the future Bismarck would want to complete German unification by incorporating the south German states into a new Reich. This would be opposed by France because it would represent a major shift in the balance of power to France's disadvantage. After Napoleon III's failure to secure territory in the Rhineland and then Luxembourg, he felt humiliated and determined not to suffer any further rebuffs at the hands of Bismarck. He therefore sought to strengthen France's position by making alliances.

- Russia, still smarting from its defeat in the Crimean war at the hands of Britain and France and from Napoleon III's support for the Polish rebels in 1863, was not interested.
- Britain would remain neutral.
- Italy would only agree to an alliance if French troops were withdrawn from Rome, a step which French public opinion would not accept.
- Austria was more interested in talking to the French but would only make an alliance if Italy did the same.

Negotiations with Austria did continue for some time, but ultimately France was left isolated.

Franco-Prussian war

Hohenzollern candidature for the Spanish throne. The event which finally led to war between Prussia and France in 1870 was, in itself, a minor incident. In 1868 there had been a revolution in Spain which had resulted in the monarch, Queen Isabella, being expelled. The new government of Spain then began to cast around in the search for a new monarch. After other candidates had turned down the offer of the Spanish throne, an approach was made to Prince Leopold of Hohenzollern-Sigmaringen, a distant relative of the King of Prussia. With the support of Wilhelm I and Bismarck, Leopold accepted the offer. The candidature would inevitably be opposed by France since the installation of a German prince on the Spanish throne would alter the balance of power even more to the disadvantage of the French. Bismarck was fully aware of this but was prepared to risk a crisis in Franco-Prussian relations. He hoped to present the French with a fait accompli by accepting the offer before the French were informed, but an administrative error led to a delay in the Prussian reply being sent. The news of the Hohenzollern candidature caused such a hostile reaction in Paris that King Wilhelm I persuaded Leopold to withdraw.

Ems telegram. Now it was Bismarck's turn to suffer a serious setback as France had secured a diplomatic triumph. The French government, however, demanded the King of Prussia's personal guarantee that the candidature would not be renewed. When the French Ambassador was received by Wilhelm I at Ems he was dealt with courteously but Wilhelm I firmly refused to give any such guarantee, feeling that his honour as a king was being questioned. An account of this meeting was then sent by telegram to Bismarck. Anxious to rescue his reputation and now convinced that war with France was unavoidable, Bismarck decided to publish an edited version of the telegram which gave the impression that the French Ambassador had been snubbed by the King. The publication of the Ems telegram was the final straw for the French government. Urged on by newspaper editors, his generals and his wife, Napoleon III declared war on Prussia on 19 July 1870.

Defeat of France. Fighting began on 4 August and within a month the French armies suffered a decisive defeat at Sedan. This battle, one of the most overwhelming defeats in modern times, resulted in the capture of over 100,000 French soldiers (including the Emperor) and the collapse of the imperial government in France. The war dragged on for a further five months, however; with the Prussian

Street fighting during the Franco-Prussian war.

armies besieging Paris, the new republican government in France kept up resistance but at the end of January 1871 the French had to bow to the inevitable and accept an armistice. A peace treaty was finally concluded at Frankfurt in May 1871. Under the terms of the Peace of Frankfurt France lost the strategically important provinces of Alsace and Lorraine to Germany and was forced to pay an indemnity of 5000 million francs. An army of occupation would remain in France until the indemnity had been paid in full.

The war had unleashed a wave of popular patriotism across Germany which put pressure on the rulers of the south German states to unite with the North German Confederation. Baden declared a wish for unification but Bavaria and Wurttemberg would only join if the King were given special privileges. These included command of their own armies in peacetime, separate diplomatic representation abroad and control of some areas of transport and taxation. After complex and skilful negotiations Bismarck succeeded in bringing the south German states into a united Germany and, on 18 January 1871, in the Hall of Mirrors at Versailles, the new German Reich was proclaimed with the King of Prussia as its Kaiser.

SUMMARY QUESTIONS

1 What were Bismarck's aims in 1862?

2 What was the significance of the Schleswig–Holstein crisis for (a) German nationalists and (b) Bismarck?

3 How did the Schleswig–Holstein crisis lead to war between Prussia and Austria?

4 What were the consequences of the Austro-Prussian war for (a) Austria, (b) Prussia and (c) other German states?

5 Why was France so alarmed by the Prussian victory over Austria?

6 Why was there a wave of German patriotic support for Prussia during its war against France?

CHAPTER 5

Politics in the German Reich, 1871–9

In the space of nine years and through three wars, Bismarck had succeeded in uniting Germany under Prussian leadership. Prussia itself had gained extensive territory in north and central Germany. A Kleindeutsch solution to German unification had been imposed on Germany leaving Austria with no influence. The German **Reich** itself was a large, new state in central Europe which had been created by force of arms and which completely altered the balance of power in Europe. Within the Reich there were large non-German minorities: the Poles in Prussia's eastern provinces, the Danes in Schleswig–Holstein and French in Alsace–Lorraine. There were also many Germans living outside the Reich, especially in Austria. For German nationalists, however, the creation of the Reich was an achievement to be celebrated, despite the fact that Bismarck's Reich was not what the members of the Frankfurt Parliament had envisaged during their attempts to unite Germany in 1848.

CONSTITUTION

In the most important respects the constitution of the new Reich was the same as the one drawn up by Bismarck for the North German Confederation in 1867.

- The Bundesrat was still made up of representatives of the princes and could still be dominated by Prussia. Although the Bundesrat was given extra powers – for example, it had to give its approval before war could be declared – these powers were rarely used by the princes to assert their independence and it was little more than a rubber stamp for approving Bismarck's policies.
- Prussia's position as the dominant state within the Reich was enshrined in the constitution. The King of Prussia was the German Kaiser; the Minister-President of

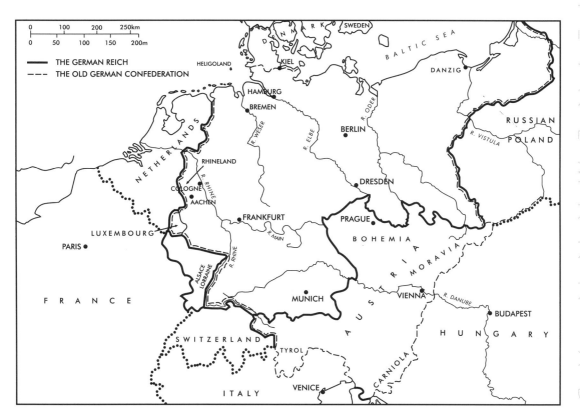

The German Reich, 1871.

Prussia was the German Chancellor and the Prussian army was the German army in war time.

- Bismarck himself occupied a pivotal position at the centre of this system of government. He controlled the governments of Prussia and the Reich. He alone, of all the ministers, appeared before the Reichstag to explain his policies. His unique relationship with the Kaiser enabled him to control all the important affairs of state and his skill as a politician and a diplomat enabled him to balance all the competing forces in this complex structure.

- As in the North German Confederation, the Reichstag in the German Reich was elected by universal male suffrage. Its powers over legislation and the budget were the same as before except that, after 1874, the Reichstag was given the right to review the military budget every seven years.

- The imperial ministers were appointed and dismissed by the Kaiser and were not accountable to the Reichstag. The Chancellor was obliged to appear before the Reichstag to explain and defend his policies but he was not obliged to act on any resolutions passed by it.

- Legislation which was initiated by the Chancellor, however, had to be passed by the Reichstag which meant that he had to ensure that a majority were prepared to support him. Bismarck recognised the need to make tactical alliances with parties in the Reichstag to ensure that legislation was passed.

As the one directly elected national institution within the constitution of the Reich, the Reichstag symbolised its unity. In other respects the constitution enshrined the particularist interests of the princes and the separate states.

- King Ludwig of Bavaria could only be persuaded to join the Reich voluntarily by being offered a bribe and the right to retain the vestiges of independence. The southern states kept their own postal and telegraph systems and Bavaria was allowed to retain its own army. In time of war, however, the Bavarian army would come under Prussian control.
- Bismarck himself was determined to retain Prussia's unique identity and the privileged position within Prussia of the Junker aristocracy. Junkers continued to dominate the Prussian civil service and the army and the three-class voting system in elections for the Prussian Landtag ensured conservative majorities were returned. Since the Prussian government was to retain control of its own internal affairs, this right had to be extended to all the states within the Reich. The states retained powers over education, justice, agriculture, church–state relations and local government.

Consolidation. After imposing the constitution on the new Reich Bismarck's next priority was to consolidate the unity of the new state by standardising its institutions.

- By 1875 a common currency had been introduced backed by a new central bank, the Reichsbank.
- The legal system was also modernised and standardised.

In pushing this legislation through the Reichstag Bismarck was able to rely on the support of the National Liberals, the largest party. In the early years of the Reich the National Liberals proved to be useful allies for Bismarck.

The relationship was very much on Bismarck's terms. Their support could not be taken for granted and occasionally Bismarck was prepared to make concessions but for him the alliance with the National Liberals was purely a matter of tactical expediency. A final settlement of the issue of control over the military budget was reached in 1874. The Septennial Law allowed the Reichstag to review the budget every seven years. This gave the Reichstag some control over military spending and therefore was a tactical retreat by Bismarck. The National Liberals, however, did not succeed with their demand for complete parliamentary control over the army.

THE KULTURKAMPF

Attack on Catholic church

After banning the **Jesuits** from Germany in 1872, Bismarck launched the **Kulturkampf** – an onslaught on the Catholic church and its political influence in Germany, especially in Prussia. In a series of laws passed between 1873 and 1875 the government sought to limit the influence of the Catholic church in education and other areas of German life.

- The May Laws of 1873 ordered that all candidates for the priesthood had to attend university for three years before training as priests and that all church appointments were subject to a veto by the state.
- In 1874, the registration of births, deaths and marriages in Prussia was removed from the church and taken over by the state.
- All states were also given the right to restrict the freedom of movement of the clergy and to expel any priests who did not comply with these orders.
- Finally, in 1875, the Prussian government was given the power to suspend state subsidies to dioceses where the clergy were resisting the new laws, and all religious orders were dissolved.

These laws were vigorously enforced by **Falk**, the Prussian Minister of Culture. Despite their repressive and illiberal nature they were supported by the National Liberals in the Reichstag and the Prussian Landtag.

Bismarck's motives. The reasons why Bismarck embarked on this campaign have been a matter for debate among historians. Although a Protestant himself, as a politician he was normally impartial in dealings with the churches. Liberals in Germany, as elsewhere, opposed the Catholic church because of its conservative influence and this conflict had been made worse by recent developments within the Catholic church itself.

The Catholic church. Under Pope Pius IX the church had resisted the political, social and cultural trends of the 19th century.

- In the 1864 Syllabus of Errors the Pope had declared the church to be opposed to liberalism, nationalism and 'recent' civilisation.
- In 1870 the enunciation of the Doctrine of Papal Infallibility stated that, when speaking on matters of morals and faith, the Pope could not teach erroneous doctrine.

These statements caused alarm among liberals and nationalists who were concerned that they might herald the start of a more militant phase in Catholic history. They feared that the Catholic church was about to embark on a campaign to support conservative political causes and to interfere in the domestic affairs of sovereign states.

Centre party. Bismarck, however, was not influenced in his decision to launch the Kulturkampf by pressure from the National Liberals nor by concerns over the doctrinal disputes within the Catholic church. It was political considerations which motivated Bismarck. A new Catholic political party, the *Zentrum* (Centre) party had been formed in 1870 to defend Catholic interests within the new Germany. The Catholics were a large minority in Germany and were particularly numerous in the south and west of the country. In 1866 the German Catholics had mostly sided with Austria and were therefore viewed with suspicion by Bismarck. Led by **Ludwig Windthorst**, a politician of great ability, the Centre party increased its support rapidly and became a major party in the Reichstag.

In defence of Catholic interests, the Centre party policy was to:

- support church schools and oppose civil marriage
- support greater decentralisation and more autonomy for the individual states (in opposition to Bismarck's efforts to consolidate and strengthen the power of the imperial government)
- support social reforms such as factory legislation, the regulation of child and female labour and the setting up of arbitration courts to settle disputes between employers and labour.

Bismarck was suspicious of the Centre party. He was alarmed at its radical social programme and convinced that a party which put religion before politics was sectarian and divisive. His view that the Centre party in particular and the Catholic church in general were a threat to the unity of the Reich was reinforced when the Centre party became a focus for opposition in the Reichstag. Deputies from the Polish provinces, from Denmark and from Alsace–Lorraine all joined together in a loose alliance with the Centre to form an opposition. Bismarck came to the view that this was a Vatican-inspired conspiracy against the new German Reich and his decision to launch the Kulturkampf was motivated by a determination to defend the Reich which he had so recently created.

Church's response. Despite the vigorous enforcement of the laws by Falk the church refused to submit. By 1876 ten of the twelve Prussian bishops were either under arrest or in exile and one-quarter of all parishes had no priest. Despite this repression the Catholic church continued to thrive and the Centre party grew in strength. In fact the Catholic church was used to dealing with persecution and could only be strengthened by it as ordinary Catholics rallied around their church and concluded that a separate Catholic political party was essential for the defence of their church.

Bismarck retreats. Realising that the campaign was going badly and facing mounting opposition from the royal family, Bismarck decided to retreat. His opportunity to do this without losing face was provided by the death of Pius IX in 1878. His successor, Leo XIII, proved to be more conciliatory and, in the summer of 1878, Bismarck began long and difficult negotiations with the Pope's envoy. The issue was not finally settled until 1887. Bismarck's Kulturkampf failed to destroy the Centre party; he had to abolish the May Laws and allow the exiled clergy to return; and state payments to the church were resumed. On the other hand, it was not a complete victory for the church. Civil marriage was still compulsory; Jesuits were still banned from Germany and the state retained the right to vet church appointments.

A TURNING POINT, 1878–9

Policy changes
In the late 1870s Bismarck initiated a series of changes in policy which had far-reaching consequences for the future direction of the German Reich. In order to make these changes he had to enter into new political alliances and abandon the political allies who had helped him in the first phase of creating and shaping the new Reich. The changes amounted to a major realignment of German politics.

* The abandonment of the Kulturkampf.
* The beginning of a new political struggle against socialism.
* The re-introduction of tariffs on the imports of foreign goods.
* The ending of Bismarck's alliance with the National Liberals and the start of a new political alignment within the Reichstag.

Economic difficulties
The background to these changes can be found in the economic and political pressures which had been building up in Germany since the early 1870s. After experiencing a rapid boom in the years immediately after the unification of Germany, the German economy suffered a serious financial crisis in 1873, followed by several years of much slower growth. German manufacturers, in the process of trying to develop their trade within their newly expanded home market, faced stiff competition from foreign manufacturers. By 1878 many of the leading German manufacturers had combined together in the Central Association of German Manufacturers to campaign for the

re-introduction of tariffs on imports to protect German producers from foreign competition. A similar process was occurring in other European states, with the exception of Great Britain.

Agriculture had also been badly hit by increased foreign competition and by a series of bad harvests at the end of the 1870s. American wheat had begun to be imported into Europe at the beginning of the 1870s; Russian wheat was also available in large quantities and at lower prices than German-grown produce. Peasant farmers and aristocratic landowners alike feared for their incomes and their survival; they began, in the same way as manufacturers, to campaign for protective tariffs to keep out imported foreign grain.

Tariff reform. As a Junker landowner himself, Bismarck was sympathetic to the demands of the agriculturalists. A threat to agricultural incomes would, in the long term, undermine the economic position of the Junker aristocracy. Bismarck was also concerned about the strategic implications of becoming dependent on imported foreign grain. A nation which could not feed itself would become more vulnerable in time of war. Tariffs would also provide the government of the Reich with much needed revenue. As the Reich government could not tax German citizens directly but had to rely on the states passing on part of their revenue to the central government, shortage of finance was a perennial problem for Bismarck. Tariffs could increase revenue directly to the central government and, because they would not be voted on annually by the Reichstag, would be outside parliamentary control.

Political realignments

Since 1867 Bismarck had relied on a loose political alliance with the National Liberal party to get his legislation passed by the Reichstag. They had been his allies in the process of unifying Germany, of modernising the institutions of the Reich and in the Kulturkampf. The relationship had been fraught with difficulty and was characterised by lack of trust on both sides, but it had served Bismarck well. The National Liberals were traditionally a free-trade party, however. Support for tariffs would come from the new German Conservative party. This party, which drew its support from aristocratic landowners and Protestant peasants, was keen to work closely with Bismarck. The Centre party, which drew the bulk of its support from Catholic small farmers and artisans, might also be prepared to support tariffs but co-operation with Bismarck was ruled out as long as the Kulturkampf was in progress. Bismarck did not rule out the possibility that the National Liberals might be flexible on this issue and offered their leader, Bennigsen, the inducement of a post in the Prussian cabinet. This was not enough for Bennigsen who demanded two additional posts. Bismarck refused and negotiations broke down completely over Bismarck's plans to establish a state monopoly over tobacco, a policy which would be totally unacceptable to liberals.

Anti-Socialist Law. The log-jam was broken by unforeseen developments.
- The death of Pope Pius IX gave Bismarck the opportunity to negotiate his way out of the Kulturkampf, a move which would allow the possibility of closer relations with the Centre party.
- In May 1878, an anarchist tried to assassinate the Kaiser. The man had no connection with the Socialist party but, in Bismarck's eyes, there was no difference between anarchism and socialism. Both were revolutionary, both a threat to the traditional social order which Bismarck was dedicated to preserving.
- Bismarck was determined to suppress the new Socialist party. He introduced a bill into the Reichstag to place severe restrictions on the freedom of the press and to make incitement to class war a criminal offence. The bill was defeated by the National Liberals and the Centre.
- A second attempt on the Kaiser's life, which left him badly wounded, gave Bismarck the opportunity to turn the situation to his advantage.
- The Reichstag was dissolved and new elections called. In the election campaign Bismarck was able to brand the National Liberals as unpatriotic for standing in the way of essential legislation to protect the Kaiser.
- The result was a serious defeat for the National Liberals, who lost 29 seats in the Reichstag, and a victory for the Conservatives. The Centre party held on to its seats and now held the balance of power in the new Reichstag.

The way was now clear for Bismarck to introduce his Anti-Socialist Law. Under the law, which was passed by the new Reichstag, socialist and communist meetings and publications were banned. The police were given the power to expel socialist agitators and the states were given the power to declare a state of siege, giving the police extraordinary powers, in disaffected areas for up to one year. A legal loophole, however, allowed the socialists still to participate in elections.

The new political balance in the Reichstag also paved the way for the introduction of tariffs. Bismarck introduced a Tariff Bill in 1879 which imposed import duties on iron, iron goods and grain. The Bill was passed by a majority made up from the Conservatives, Free Conservatives, Centre and part of the National Liberal party. It was a great political triumph for Bismarck and one which, in the process of being achieved, transformed German politics for the remainder of his time in power.

RESULTS OF THE POLITICAL CHANGES

The effects of the political crisis of 1878–9 were as follows.

- Although agricultural prices continued to fall, the tariff on grain protected farmers and landowners from the worst effects of the agricultural depression. Landowners became staunch supporters of Bismarck during the 1880s.
- Owners of large industrial enterprises also abandoned their support for free trade and therefore their support for the National Liberal party. In the 1880s leading industrialists supported the Conservative party in the so-called 'alliance of steel and rye'.
- The National Liberal party never recovered from the strains of the tariff-reform crisis. There were already divisions in the party before 1878 and the party lacked the broad-based appeal and the local organisation to survive in a parliamentary system based on universal suffrage. The party split in 1879. The right wing of the party supported Bismarck over tariff reform and the Anti-Socialist Law but in the 1880s this group was but a

shadow of its former self. The free-trade supporters broke away and joined the more radical Progressive party. Liberalism as a political force in Germany was dying.

- The German Reich became more united as a result of tariffs, but around a more conservative political agenda. The alliance of steel and rye was an expression of this political consolidation. Bismarck presented tariffs as a patriotic necessity, essential for the defence of the Fatherland.

- Consumers suffered from artificially high prices, especially on basic food products such as bread. By favouring producers over consumers, Bismarck's tariffs had the effect of reducing living standards, especially for the very poor. This had long-term consequences for German society as social unrest was increased.

- Bismarck had demonstrated his power over the Reichstag and his ability to make and break alliances. In the 1880s he relied for his majorities in the Reichstag on an alliance between the Conservative parties and the Centre, together with the right wing of the National Liberal party.

SUMMARY QUESTIONS

1 How did the Reich constitution of 1871 preserve the power of the monarchy?

2 What were the liberal aspects of the constitution?

3 Why was Bismarck so concerned by the rise of the Centre party?

4 Who gained and who lost from the Kulturkampf?

5 What were Bismarck's motives in introducing tariffs in 1879? Which was his most important motive? Give reasons for your answer.

6 What were (a) the economic and (b) the political consequences of Bismarck's policy changes in the years 1878–9?

CHAPTER 6

Economic and social change, 1871–90

One of the driving forces behind the unification of Germany in the years before 1870 was the expansion of trade and industry across the frontiers of the separate states and the growth of a middle class which could see unification as bringing positive economic benefits to the business world. After unification, which created a large internal market within the new Reich, German industry continued to grow and to expand its trade with the outside world. This expansion of industry and the wealth it created helped to lay the foundations for the growing military power of the Reich. Economic change, however, also stimulated far-reaching changes in German society.

INDUSTRIAL EXPANSION

The rapid growth in output, which had been a feature of the German economy in the 1850s and 1860s, continued until 1873. In that year German businesses, in common with those in other industrialised nations, suffered a serious slump in which many companies failed, prices began to fall, unemployment began to rise and wages were forced down. In the view of some economic historians, the collapse of 1873 was the start of a 'Great Depression' which lasted until 1896. In some respects it is true that the economic conditions in which businesses were operating were less favourable in this period than they had been in the previous twenty years. Prices continued to fall and profits were reduced. On the other hand, industrial output had recovered to its 1873 level by 1876 and thereafter continued to rise. Between 1870 and 1890 the output of the key commodities of an industrialised nation – coal, iron and steel – all increased by leaps and bounds. Coal output, for example, more than doubled; pig-iron production increased by almost three times; and steel production showed a phenomenal rate of expansion, growing by a factor of almost thirteen. The main German centres of industry at this time, especially the Ruhr valley and Silesia, were booming.

New industries. Germany also became a world leader in the newer chemical and electrical industries. The Germans had significant advantages in these fields which were exploited to the full. Technical and science education in Germany was given a higher priority than in many other countries, notably Great Britain. In 1870, for example, there were more science graduates at just one German university – Munich – than the total number of science graduates from all English universities. Germany had abundant reserves of coal and potash which became the basis for numerous chemical products which were discovered by German scientists in the last decades of the 19th century. By the 1890s Germany had established a virtual world monopoly in the production of synthetic dyes, artificial fibres, some photographic materials, some drugs, plastics and new explosives. In the electrical field, also, German firms such

A Krupp steel breechloader of the 1870s, designed to fire 1000lb shells.

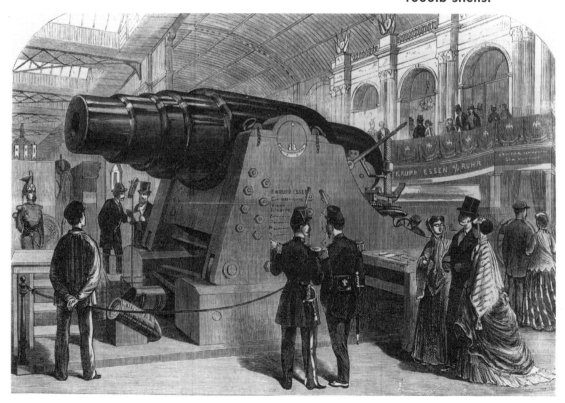

KEY STATISTICS

KEY STATISTICS

German coal production

1871	37.9m tons
1880	59.1m tons
1890	89.1m tons

German pig-iron production

1870	1.4m tons
1880	2.7m tons
1890	4.0m tons

German steel production

1870	169,000 tons
1880	660,000 tons
1890	2,161,000 tons

as Siemens were leading the way in the production of such things as dynamos.

Cartels. One notable feature of this phase of Germany's industrial expansion was the emergence of cartels. As companies grew in size, a relatively small number of companies were able to exercise a disproportionate influence over the market. Federations of the leading firms within an industry – or cartels – could take this process one step further by establishing a monopoly position through which they were able to control prices. In the trading conditions of this period, with growing international competition and generally falling prices, the pressure to create cartels was almost overwhelming and, indeed, the process was encouraged by the government. In 1875 there were eight cartels in Germany; by 1885 there were about 90. These federations of firms gave manufacturers considerable power within the market place but they also increased their political influence. Pressure for tariffs to protect German manufacturers by artificially raising prices was exerted by the cartels.

AGRICULTURE

After 1873 there was a long-term decline in agricultural prices and, consequently, in the incomes of farmers and landowners. This situation was exacerbated by the series of bad harvests in the late 1870s. The building of new railways and roads broke down the isolation of rural communities and exposed farmers to competition from outside. The result was that a growing number of peasants abandoned agriculture and moved to the industrial towns. On the other hand, the growth of the towns and the protection given to German grain growers after 1879 did create opportunities for the more enterprising farmers to supply food to a growing domestic market. Farm machinery and fertilisers were beginning to become available and those farmers who had the money to invest in such innovations could, and did, raise their yields considerably. More than 4 million acres of land were brought under cultivation between 1880 and 1900.

SOCIAL CHANGES

Urbanisation. Germany experienced rapid population growth during these years, rising from approximately 41 million in 1871 to over 49 million in 1890. There was also significant internal migration of the population. In 1871 nearly 64 per cent of the population lived in the countryside but by 1890 this figure had fallen to 57.5 per cent and would continue to fall over the next twenty years. Although Germany still had a much higher proportion of its population living in rural areas and working in agriculture than other industrialised nations such as Great Britain, the trend towards a more urban society was clear.

- Many peasants left their farms for the towns even though they did not travel more than a few miles from their birthplaces.
- Many moved from the eastern provinces of Prussia to Berlin and the industrial towns of the Ruhr valley.
- Even in the 1860s two-thirds of the adult male population of Berlin had been born outside the city.
- The Krupp factories in Essen attracted thousands of peasants' sons, forced to leave their family farms by the decline of peasant agriculture.
- In Bochum, a town which was almost entirely the creation of the industrial revolution, the needs for labour were met by a large-scale influx of Polish peasants from Prussia's eastern provinces.

Middle class. New wealth was being generated very rapidly in the growing industrial cities and the main beneficiaries of this process were the middle class. For the dynamic entrepreneur there was a great deal of money to be made and people like Werner Siemens, Emil Rathenau, August Thyssen, William Cuno and Carl Furstenberg built up great industrial, commercial and financial empires. The middle class, in general, experienced a long-term upward trend in their incomes which was reflected in the building of comfortable middle-class homes and the rise of the large department stores catering for a largely middle-class clientele. Some chose to spend their wealth on ostentatious country homes that could rival the grand mansions of the aristocracy in their size and opulence. The Krupps, for example, built their Villa Hugel in the 1870s on the

Population growth

1871	41.05m
1880	42.23m
1890	49.42m

KEY STATISTICS

The growth of cities

	1875	1890
Berlin	967,000	1.588m
Dusseldorf	81,000	145,000
Hamburg	265,000	324,000
Munich	193,000	349,000
Leipzig	127,000	295,000

southern fringe of Essen. The Oppenheim family from Berlin bought a country estate in Pomerania and adopted the aristocratic title of the 'Oppenheims zu Rheinfeld'. This process of upward social mobility for the middle class could be seen in the increase in the number of middle-class officers within the army, traditionally an exclusively aristocratic preserve. There were, however, limits to social advancement for the middle class. Elite regiments in the army retained an aristocratic monopoly within their officer corps. The civil service was still dominated by the Junkers and, in social and political life, the Junker elite maintained the barriers between aristocracy and 'nouveau riches'.

Working class. At the other end of the social scale life for the growing working class in the industrial cities had few of the benefits deriving from the rapid creation of wealth. The raw statistics showing a long-term rising trend in the value of real wages indicate that, in general, the German working class did experience an increase in their living standards in the last decades of the 19th century. These figures, however, disguise the fact that there were wide variations in wage levels – coal miners, for example, tended to be better paid than many others – and that there were a large number of families whose standard of living was below the poverty line. The cities grew so rapidly in many cases that, in the short term, there was a desperate housing shortage.

- In Berlin in 1871, for example, 10,000 people were classified as homeless.
- Most working-class families had to spend about 25 per cent of their income on accommodation, for which they received a one or two-roomed flat.
- Working conditions were equally brutal: a ten or twelve-hour day, six days per week, was the norm in conditions that were often unhealthy and dangerous.
- In the 1880s in Germany's larger cities the average life expectancy was below 40 years.

Within this overall picture, however, there were variations. Some employers such as the Krupps of Essen were more enlightened and provided welfare benefits for their employees.

The countryside. Although the pace of change was much slower in the countryside than in the cities, even in the villages and small towns of the rural heartland society was undergoing change. The problems of agriculture have already been mentioned and the effects of the difficulties experienced by farmers were felt by landowners also, although in different degrees.

Landowners. Economically, the position of the Junker landowners was being undermined during the last quarter of the 19th century. Falling incomes from agriculture led to growing indebtedness for many Junker families. The smaller the estate, and the further east it was situated, the greater the level of debt. The result was that many Junker landowners were forced to sell their estates, either to the newly rich middle-class families from the cities or, in Prussia's eastern provinces, to Polish landowners. So alarmed was the Prussian government at the number of estates which were being bought by Poles that in 1886 a fund was established to purchase bankrupt German estates and sell them to German migrants. Another sign of the Junkers' economic difficulties was the growing level of tax evasion by landowners, a practice which was more common in the eastern provinces than elsewhere.

Junker predominance. The political and social predominance of the Junkers, however, remained as strong as ever. On the great estates in east Prussia the hierarchy of the pre-industrial age remained in place, supported by the legal rights and privileges of the Junkers. Local government was in the hands of an appointed official, the *Landrat*, who was always the son of a Junker who had gained a degree in law. Tax evasion went largely unchecked because these officials could be relied upon to show favouritism to their relatives. Their political influence was also maintained. As late as the early 1900s the Prussian Landtag contained 161 representatives from a landowning background and only 17 from trade and industry.

Peasants. Peasants and rural artisans were among the worst casualties of the economic changes that occurred during this period. The size of Germany and the variations between the regions make generalisations difficult to sustain but the rural depopulation which affected all areas of the country reflected the struggle for peasant farmers to make a living out of agriculture. Although **feudal dues** were a thing of the past many peasants were still indebted to their landlords through compensation payments. On the great estates there was no chance of social mobility. Peasants stayed in their places and the only escape from this rigid hierarchical structure was to move away. Although railways and roads reached into rural Germany and brought outside influences and factory-made goods, rural isolation was still a feature of the more remote areas of eastern Prussia, Wurttemberg and Bavaria in the south. As late as 1910, 40 per cent of the population lived in closely-knit communities of fewer than 2000 people. Local and regional loyalties remained strong.

THE CONSEQUENCES OF SOCIAL AND ECONOMIC CHANGE

- In the growing industrial cities and in the coal-mining regions, the effect of poor working conditions and unhealthy living conditions was the growth of social unrest. One indicator of this phenomenon was the rise of the trade-union movement; another was the increase in support for the new Socialist party. Both of these movements provided a means through which the industrial working class could make an impact on Germany's political life.
- Independent farmers and rural craftworkers were among other groups which suffered from the economic changes of these years. Priding themselves on their industriousness, their sobriety and their piety, they were left feeling bewildered and discontented by the undermining of their economic position caused by falling prices and the influx of cheap, factory-made goods. Until the 1880s these people, especially those who were Protestants living in northern Germany, had voted for the National Liberal party, but these ties were beginning to weaken. By the 1890s a new social and political phenomenon, the **Mittelstand**, had begun to make its presence felt in Germany.

- In the 1880s, also, Germany experienced the rise of anti-Semitism as a distinct political force. Many of the victims of the agricultural depression and of the industrial revolution focused on the Jews as the cause of their difficulties. In the 1880s, about 45 per cent the banking system was owned by Jews. Many of the chain stores with which small shopkeepers had to compete were owned by Jews. Many of the horse dealers with whom peasant farmers did business were Jewish, as were some of the prominent politicians within the National Liberal party. Jewish entrepreneurs were increasingly accused of profiteering from the agricultural depression. Some sections of the press played upon these prejudices. In Wurttemberg, for example, Catholic newspapers would print the names of any Jew who had been found guilty of a criminal offence in bold type. Although anti-Semitism as a political force did not make its full presence felt until the 1890s, the foundations of this were being laid in the 1880s.

SUMMARY QUESTIONS

1 What factors helped to make Germany a world leader in the chemical and electrical industries?

2 Which groups benefited most from social and economic change?

3 Which groups suffered the most from social and economic change?

4 How successfully did the Junker landowners protect their positions during this period of change?

CHAPTER 7

Bismarck's anti-socialist campaign, 1878–90

THE ANTI-SOCIALIST LAW OF 1878

Bismarck's decision to introduce a law placing severe restrictions on the Socialist party in 1878 was referred to in Chapter 5. This law removed the right of socialists to hold meetings, to publish newspapers or periodicals or even to maintain a party organisation. The police were given the power to expel agitators from an area where a 'minor state of siege' had been declared and any person found guilty of breaking these regulations could be punished by a heavy fine or a prison sentence. The law did not, however, prevent the socialists from participating in elections.

Bismarck's motives. The opportunity to introduce the Anti-Socialist Law was provided by the two assassination attempts on the Kaiser in 1878. Although neither of the would-be assassins was linked to the Socialist party in any way, Bismarck made no distinction in his mind between anarchism, the political creed to which the perpetrators did subscribe, and **socialism**. In any event, the public alarm at the threat to the Kaiser was too good an opportunity for Bismarck to miss and, in the election campaign of 1878, he showed great skill in using his press connections to whip up anti-socialist feeling. Ever since the early 1870s, Bismarck had felt a growing sense of alarm at the rise of socialism in Germany. During the war against France leading socialists such as **Bebel** had opposed the annexation of Alsace–Lorraine and had supported the Paris Commune. Bismarck viewed the internationalism and the belief in class conflict on the part of the socialists as being a threat to the unity and stability of the Reich. He was disturbed by the progress made by the socialists in Reichstag elections since 1871 and the growing circulation of socialist newspapers. Bismarck's outlook on German society was essentially rooted in the past; the society he was trying to preserve was one in which the mass of the people – the peasants – would show respect and deference to the monarchy, army and Junker aristocracy. The rise of the industrial cities, with an increasingly discontented and disaffected working class, threatened to undermine the social stability of Germany. Bismarck was convinced that the 'red menace' of socialism did represent a fundamental threat to the social and political order, not only in Germany but also in the rest of Europe.

THE DEVELOPMENT OF THE SOCIALIST MOVEMENT

Workers' movements had first appeared in Germany in the 1840s, when their membership was confined to the artisans. These groups had played a part in the revolution of 1848 and, in the aftermath of the failure of the revolution, they had been suppressed. In the more liberal German states such as Baden workers' groups began to emerge again in the late 1850s. In 1863 an important step forward was made when the various small groups agreed to combine into the General German Workers' Association (ADAV). This group, led by **Ferdinand Lassalle**, adopted a programme which included the socialist aims of the redistribution of wealth and the abolition of private property. Lassalle, however, parted company with the leading socialist intellectual of the time, Karl Marx, in rejecting the Marxist belief in revolution as the only way to achieve social change. Lassalle, who was impressed with the power of the Prussian state, believed that social change could be achieved through an alliance with the state.

The SPD. In 1869 a new, more Marxist, organisation was founded. At a conference at Eisenach, **Liebknecht** and Bebel emerged as the leaders of the Social Democratic German Workers' party (SDAP) which adopted a revolutionary programme, committed to the abolition of class rule. Both organisations grew slowly so that by 1875 the ADAV had a membership of about 15,000 and the SDAP about 9000. In the wake of the economic crisis of 1873, with its resulting rise in unemployment, the socialist organisations came to realise that their ability to defend

August Bebel, leader of the SPD.

KEY STATISTICS

The growth of the SPD: seats won in Reichstag elections

1877	13
1878	9
1884	24
1887	11
1890	35

working-class interests was severely hampered by the rivalry and competition between them. In 1875, therefore, the two groups merged at a conference held at Gotha. This conference established a new party, known simply as the German Social Democratic party (SPD). The SPD affirmed its commitment to the Marxist tenets of class conflict and the necessity for the overthrow of the existing system, but it also declared its willingness to work within the existing system for short-term reforms such as a state-funded education system, universal suffrage in all German states and social legislation to protect the working conditions and health of workers.

Electoral success. In Reichstag elections the Social Democrats began to make slow but steady progress during the 1870s. From a starting point of two deputies in 1871, the SDAP grew to nine seats in 1874 and the united SPD achieved thirteen seats in 1877, winning nearly half-a-million votes. In comparison with the main political parties, the Social Democratic representation was still tiny but this did not prevent Bismarck from viewing the movement as a serious potential threat.

Trade unions. Associated with the growth of the Social Democratic party was the emergence of trade unionism in Germany's growing industrial workforce. Although still in its infancy in the mid-1870s, the trade-union movement has been estimated to have attracted about 50,000 members. There were also the so-called *Hirsch-Dunker* unions which were associated with the Liberal parties and operated more as welfare organisations than as genuine trade unions committed to wage bargaining.

THE EFFECTIVENESS OF THE ANTI-SOCIALIST LAW

The Anti-Socialist Law was enforced vigorously by the police and caused severe problems for the party and its supporters.

- Membership of the SPD declined as many fringe supporters were deterred from continuing their membership.

- The trade unions were virtually crushed, although the law was not applied to the Hirsch-Dunker unions.
- 45 of the 47 party newspapers, including their leading publication *Forward*, were suppressed.
- The Prussian government imposed a minor state of siege in Berlin in 1879 under which the police arrested and expelled 67 leading socialists from the city. This severely disrupted the party's activities in the city. This was then repeated in the Silesian city of Breslau.
- Minor states of siege were imposed in Hamburg in 1880 and Leipzig in 1881. Over 100 socialists were expelled from Hamburg and many emigrated to the United States to escape the persecution.
- Before the election of 1881 the police stepped up their activities against the Social Democrats and 600 were arrested. The SPD had so much difficulty in finding enough candidates to contest the elections that Bebel had to stand in 35 constituencies and Liebknecht in sixteen.
- In the 1881 elections the SPD vote was cut by one-third. The Social Democrat vote in Berlin dropped dramatically, partly due to the activities of the police but also because of competition from the anti-Semitic Christian Social Workers' party led by Adolf Stoecker.

Growth and development of the socialist movement

Despite these difficulties, however, the SPD not only survived but even began to make progress during the years when the Anti-Socialist Law was in force. This was shown by the election results during the period 1881–90. It was also evident in the revival of trade unionism in the late 1880s. There was a series of strikes in the industrial and mining areas in 1889 and 1890 and it is estimated that the membership of free trade unions had grown to 278,000 by 1890. Clearly the anti-socialist campaign launched by Bismarck had failed in its primary objective of crushing the movement. There were a number of reasons for this.

- The leaders, Liebknecht and Bebel, managed to rally the party and organise resistance. They were forced to clarify their policies. Particularly important in this respect was the decision in 1880 to reject anarchist and terrorist tactics and to commit themselves to all other means of resistance.

- A new party newspaper, the *Social Democrat*, was published in Zurich and smuggled over the border into Germany. The party developed a sophisticated postal system of its own to distribute its publications to members, an essential device for keeping the members in different parts of the country informed about policies and the progress of the various branches.
- Secret conferences were organised on foreign soil. The first was in Switzerland in 1880, followed by Denmark in 1883 and Switzerland again in 1887.
- The experience of persecution led the Social Democrats to develop great loyalty and solidarity, just as the Catholics had done during the Kulturkampf of the 1870s. The party offered its members more than just the opportunity to participate in politics. It ran its own educational courses, libraries, sports clubs and even choral societies. In the view of one historian the SPD created its own 'alternative culture' to bind its members more closely together.
- New electoral organisations, called 'societies for municipal elections' were set up in the large cities so that the SPD could participate legally in political activity and rebuild its local organisations.

STATE SOCIALISM

Bismarck's efforts to crush socialism were not confined to negative repression. He was also concerned to demonstrate to working-class voters that the state had more to offer the working class than the SPD. He therefore began a programme of social reforms that addressed some of the problems faced by working-class families.

- In 1883 he introduced a scheme of medical insurance, covering 3 million workers and their families. Under this scheme, which was paid for jointly by employers and employees, medical bills for workers and their families would be paid.
- In 1884 an accident insurance scheme was introduced, financed entirely by employers. This provided benefits

and funeral grants to people who had been injured at work.
- In 1886 the accident insurance scheme was extended to cover 7 million agricultural workers.
- In 1889 old age pensions were introduced for people over the age of 70.

These reforms, often referred to as a 'programme of state socialism' were intended by Bismarck to wean working-class voters away from the SPD. They did place the Social Democratic leaders in something of a dilemma. On the one hand, Bismarck's intentions were clear; his reforms would strengthen the power of the state and could also soften the militancy of the working class. On the other hand, outright opposition would create the impression that the party was obstructing reforms which could bring genuine immediate benefits to the working class. The SPD, therefore, decided to try to amend the legislation in the Reichstag to increase the benefits to the working class and then, once reforms had been passed, the party claimed credit for the fact that Bismarck had been forced to introduce it at all.

Bismarck's hope that repression and reforms would stem the tide of Social Democrat success was proved unfounded. Save in the election of 1887, when Bismarck used a war scare with France to persuade voters to rally around the Kaiser and the Fatherland, the SPD increased its vote and its representation in the Reichstag in all the elections between 1881 and 1890. Bismarck's anti-socialist campaign was clearly a failure.

SUMMARY QUESTIONS

1 Why was Bismarck so alarmed by the rise of socialism?

2 How effective was the Anti-Socialist Law in practice?

3 What were Bismarck's motives in introducing 'a programme of state socialism'?

CHAPTER 8

Bismarck's foreign policy, 1871–90

THE CHALLENGE

In 1871 Bismarck had completed the process of German unification which he had begun in 1862. The German Reich had been created through victories in three wars in the space of six years. During the course of these events there had been a decisive shift in the balance of power in Europe. The Austrian Empire had been defeated and, in order to preserve what was left of his Empire, Franz Josef had made a compromise with the Hungarians to create the Austro-Hungarian Empire. The French Empire had also been defeated and its Emperor, Napoleon III, was overthrown as a result. France now had a republican government. In the conduct of German foreign policy, which was very much under his personal control, Bismarck

Europe, 1871.

had to deploy all his skill as a diplomat and a politician to preserve the Reich he had helped to create.

Bismarck declared in 1871 that Germany was now a 'satiated' power; the Reich had no further territorial demands on any other state and would concentrate in future on holding on to the territory that had been gained during unification. In foreign-policy terms this meant that Bismarck would henceforth be working to maintain the peace and defend the status quo in Europe. The greatest danger to the Reich that could arise was if one of the defeated powers, Austria–Hungary or France, should seek a war of revenge and especially if either of them were to find an ally. In France there was a strong desire for *revanche* (revenge) and an unwillingness to accept the loss of Alsace-Lorraine. A war on two fronts would pose far greater dangers than Prussia had faced in either of the conflicts of 1866 and 1870. Bismarck's diplomacy was directed towards avoiding this eventuality and, in particular, at trying to ensure that France should remain isolated.

KEY TERM

Revanchisme The desire for *revanche* (revenge) became a factor in French politics after the defeat of 1871. The particular focus for this sentiment was the ambition to regain the lost territories of Alsace and Lorraine.

The situation facing Bismarck in 1871 was favourable. France was still recovering from defeat, as was Austria–Hungary. The Austro-Hungarian Empire was also beginning to shift its interest away from Germany and Italy towards south-east Europe and the Balkans. Russia was involved in expansion in Central Asia. Great Britain was going through an isolationist phase in its foreign policy. There were, therefore, no immediate dangers of a hostile coalition of powers being formed against Germany, but Bismarck was fully aware that these circumstances would not last forever. France would recover and would try to end its isolation. Either Austria–Hungary or Russia might emerge as a potential future ally of France.

Dreikaiserbund, 1873

The *Dreikaiserbund* (Three Emperors' League) was a loose coalition of Germany, Austria–Hungary and Russia which began in 1873. Between Austria–Hungary and Russia there was growing mistrust and antagonism arising out of the situation in the Balkans. This mistrust had the potential to lead to conflict in the future. In the event of such a conflict either of the two powers might look to Germany as a possible ally, placing Bismarck in the position of having to choose between them. This carried the danger for Germany that whichever of the two powers was rejected by Germany might then turn to France as an alternative ally. In order to avoid having to make such a choice Bismarck used the *Dreikaiserbund*, which was essentially a symbolic gesture on the part of the three rulers, as a device for containing the rivalry between Austria–Hungary and Russia and for keeping France isolated. The three Emperors stressed their desire for peace and agreed to consult each other before taking any unilateral action which could lead to war. They also declared their determination to defend monarchies against the revolutionary forces of republicanism and socialism.

'War in Sight' crisis, 1875

France recovered from its defeat in 1871 much more quickly than Bismarck had anticipated. The heavy indemnity which France had to pay Germany was paid by 1873 and the French army was being rapidly reorganised and strengthened. Bismarck became alarmed at the prospect of a revitalised France and tried to intimidate the French by organising a press campaign raising the prospect of another war. One article appeared in the Berlin newspaper, *Die Post*, under the headline 'Is War in Sight?' Bismarck also banned the export of German horses to France, a step normally taken as a preparation for war. He had no intention of actually going to war; he was merely trying to make France believe that Germany would do so unless France abandoned the rearmament programme. The plan was a serious miscalculation on Bismarck's part. Other powers became alarmed at the prospect of another European war. Britain, Italy and Russia expressed their concerns to the government in Berlin and the Russian Tsar demanded assurances that there would be no attack upon France. Bismarck gave the necessary assurances.

Bismarck was furious. He had been outmanoeuvred by the Russian Foreign Minister, suffered a diplomatic defeat and, far from isolating France, he had provoked other powers into rallying to the side of the French in order to prevent Germany becoming the dominant power in Europe.

THE EASTERN CRISIS, 1875–8

A renewed outbreak of conflict and instability in the Balkans posed serious problems for Bismarck's strategy of maintaining good working relations with both Austria–Hungary and Russia simultaneously. The crisis began in 1875 with a revolt against Turkish rule in Bosnia and Herzegovina. The revolt spread to Bulgaria in 1876; with Turkish power in the region seemingly collapsing, Serbia and Montenegro then declared war on Turkey.

Germany at this stage had no vital interests at stake in the Balkans but the crisis there nevertheless posed serious potential risks for German foreign policy. If the Turkish Empire should collapse, the resulting power vacuum in the Balkans would lead to growing rivalry and conflict between Austria–Hungary and Russia as each power sought to establish dominance in the region. Both powers would look to Germany for support and Bismarck would have to make a choice between them. Whichever power was thus rejected would then, almost inevitably, turn to France.

In the early stages of this crisis, Bismarck was fortunate that Austria–Hungary and Russia were able to co-operate. In 1876 they agreed that, in the event of a Turkish collapse, they would partition the Balkans between themselves. They were also able to throw their joint weight behind a British proposal to put pressure on the Turkish government to introduce reforms in its Empire which would satisfy some of the demands of the subject nations. Co-operation, however, could not survive indefinitely.

Russian intervention. The Turks were able to suppress the revolts and to defeat both Serbia and Montenegro. Their methods, however, led to international condemnation. During the Bulgarian revolt Turkish forces massacred over 12,000 inhabitants. The Turks also rejected international pressure to introduce internal reforms. Under pressure from the growing **pan-Slavist** movement in Russia, the Tsar decided to intervene. Even at this stage the Russians still had the agreement of Austria–Hungary for its military intervention as long as Russia confined the conflict to the

KEY CONCEPT

Pan-Slavism. This was a racial doctrine which stressed the common heritage of the Slav peoples of Europe, e.g. Russians, Poles, Czechs, Slovaks, Serbs, Bulgarians etc. Pan-Slavism promoted the idea of Russian leadership of the Slav peoples and was therefore a useful support for the expansion of Russian influence.

(a)

(b)

(c)

(a) The Balkans in 1870.

(b) The Balkans after the Treaty of San Stefano, March 1878.

(c) The Balkans after the Treaty of Berlin, July 1878.

eastern Balkans and Austria would receive Bosnia and Herzegovina in any peace settlement.

Treaty of San Stefano. In April 1877 Russia declared war on Turkey. By January 1878 Turkey had been defeated and in March 1878 the Treaty of San Stefano was imposed by Russia. This created a large, new, independent state, – Bulgaria, which would almost certainly become a satellite state of Russia in the region. This was in breach of the spirit of the agreement with Austria–Hungary and also invoked British protests on the grounds that it was a major boost to Russia's strategic position in the region. The British Prime Minister, Disraeli, threatened Russia with war unless the Treaty were revised.

Congress of Berlin. Bismarck now faced the very situation he had been trying since 1871 to avoid. To avert a war in which Austria–Hungary and Russia would be fighting one another, he proposed a Congress of all the powers in Berlin and offered his services as an 'honest broker' who would chair the meetings and act with scrupulous fairness. The outcome of the Congress was a serious diplomatic defeat for Russia which was forced to agree to Bulgaria being significantly reduced in size. Austrian troops were to occupy Bosnia and Herzegovina; Britain gained Cyprus.

The Russian delegation left Berlin highly dissatisfied and blaming Bismarck for their defeat. Although Bismarck had been impartial in his role as chair, the fact that he had not been prepared to put pressure on Austria–Hungary was interpreted by the Russians as an anti-Russian act. Influential Russians complained that the Congress had been a 'European coalition against Russia under the leadership of Prince Bismarck'. One of the major casualties of the Eastern crisis of 1875–8 was the *Dreikaiserbund* which had now fallen apart.

Dual Alliance (Germany and Austria-Hungary), 1879

Once it became clear to Bismarck that the Russians had no interest in renewing the *Dreikaiserbund*, he began to work on the idea of an alliance with Austria–Hungary. Relations with Russia were continuing to deteriorate as Bismarck's decision to impose tariffs on imported grain in 1879 hit

Russian grain producers very hard; the Russian Tsar warned the Kaiser of the potential consequences of Bismarck's policies which were perceived as anti-Russian. Bismarck, therefore, had to use all his powers of persuasion, including a threat to resign, to convince the Kaiser that an alliance with Austria–Hungary was necessary and desirable. He argued that the alliance would help to stabilise the situation in the Balkans, prevent German isolation and put pressure on Russia to agree to a new *Dreikaiserbund*.

The alliance was signed in October 1879. It was a defensive alliance which would last for five years. It stipulated that if either power were attacked by Russia the other would come to the support of its ally; if either were attacked by any other power, however, its ally would merely observe a position of 'benevolent neutrality'. Germany now had a firm alliance, but the anti-Russian tone of the alliance risked driving Russia into seeking an alliance with France.

Three Emperors' Alliance, 1881

Having been isolated by the signing of the Dual Alliance, the Russians did not immediately abandon efforts to maintain good relations with Germany. Indeed, as Bismarck had calculated, the formation of the Dual Alliance did put pressure on the Russians to seek a revival of the Dreikaiserbund but on very different terms. The result was the Three Emperors' Alliance (or *Dreikaiserbundnis*) which was concluded in 1881. Under the terms of this Alliance, Austria agreed to the eventual reunification of Bulgaria, Russia gave consent to the eventual annexation of Bosnia and Herzegovina by Austria–Hungary and all three powers agreed that, in the event of one of them being involved in war with a fourth power, the other two would adopt a position of benevolent neutrality.

The Three Emperors' Alliance fulfilled Bismarck's objectives of maintaining good relations with Austria–Hungary and Russia simultaneously and avoiding having to make a final choice between the two rival powers. Although the Alliance was an attempt to manage the conflict in the Balkans it provided no long-term solutions to the problem of Austro-Russian rivalry. Moreover, Bismarck could have no control over the direction of Russian foreign policy which was becoming increasingly unstable. A new and inexperienced Tsar, Alexander III, was receiving conflicting advice. His Foreign Minister, Giers, proposed a pro-German policy whilst other influential pan-Slavist advisers were allowed to begin intrigues in the Balkans which were bound to lead to conflict with Austria–Hungary and its German ally.

The Three Emperors' Alliance was renewed in 1884 but continuing tensions between Austria–Hungary and Russia over Bulgaria in 1885–6 destroyed it.

Triple Alliance, 1882

Italian unification had been completed in 1870. Italy still had claims on Austrian territory in the southern Tyrol and in Croatia which meant that, if Austria–Hungary should ever be involved in a war with Russia, an Italian attack on its southern frontier could not be ruled out. In the early 1880s, however, Italian anger was mainly directed against France after the French occupied the north African territory of Tunis.

Bismarck took advantage of these tensions to enlarge the Dual Alliance by bringing in Italy in 1882. The terms of the Triple Alliance favoured Italy because Germany and Austria–Hungary promised to support the Italians in the event of a French attack. Austria–Hungary also gained, however, because there was no longer any prospect of an Italian attack on the Empire in the event of a war with Russia. Austria–Hungary's position was further strengthened when Serbia was included in the Alliance in 1882 and Romania in 1885. These additions created a defensive block against Russian expansion in the Balkans.

GERMAN COLONIAL EMPIRE, 1884–5

In the 1870s and early 1880s the pace of European colonial expansion in Africa and the Pacific had greatly increased. Great Britain and France were the two powers

KEY FACTS

German Empire. Bismarck's decision to acquire colonies in 1884 was also motivated by short-term, domestic, political considerations. Empire building was a useful device for encouraging the growth of patriotic sentiment. In the election of 1884 the drive for a new overseas empire gave the conservative parties a nationalistic issue with which to combat the growing strength of the SPD.

Kolonialverein. The Colonial Union, founded in 1882, campaigned for Germany to have an overseas empire. Although it only had 9000 members in 1884, it had large funds donated by banks and major companies and had an influence out of all proportion to its size.

German colonies in Africa.

most involved in the so-called 'scramble for Africa' but other minor powers such as Portugal and Italy were staking their claims to African territory. Before 1884 Bismarck had shown no apparent interest in acquiring an overseas **German Empire** and indeed had dismissed colonies as expensive luxuries. In 1884, however, he made an abrupt change of policy. Under pressure from the successful pressure group, the **Kolonialverein**, and from German merchants with commercial interests in Africa and the Pacific, Bismarck decided in 1884 to establish protectorates over territory in south-west Africa, the Cameroons and Togoland in west Africa and New Guinea in the Pacific. The following year Germany established a protectorate over Zanzibar and part of east Africa.

Involvement in the scramble for Africa inevitably affected Germany's relations with other European powers, particularly Britain and France. Indeed, Bismarck almost certainly calculated that this would provide an opportunity to drive a wedge between Britain and France and might even lead to closer relations between Germany and France. He was, therefore, careful to support French claims against Britain over Egypt. Anglo-German relations became strained but, with no allies and many disputes with rival powers, Britain was in no position to resist German colonial expansion: an Anglo-German Agreement of 1886 endorsed British acceptance of Germany's acquisitions.

In establishing protectorates Bismarck was careful to leave the administration of the territories in the hands of private trading companies, thereby saving the government much expense. In practice, many of the costs of administering the territories fell upon the German government whilst the expected financial gains did not materialise. Bismarck rapidly became disillusioned with colonial expansion and there were no further acquisitions after 1885.

Reinsurance Treaty, 1887

With the revival of tension in the Balkans over **Bulgaria** in 1885, the Three Emperors' Alliance was again placed under strain. The Tsar refused to renew the Alliance in 1887 but agreed to negotiate with Germany alone. The result was the Reinsurance Treaty by which Bismarck agreed, in secret, to support Russia's claims in Bulgaria, a commitment which breached the spirit of the Dual Alliance with Austria. The two powers also agreed to remain neutral in the event of one of them fighting a war against any third power, except if Russia were to attack Austria or Germany were to attack France.

This agreement was very limited in its scope and Bismarck did not attach much importance to it; its value lay in the fact that Russia was still involved in a formal agreement with Germany and was therefore less likely to be interested in an alliance with France. Relations between Germany and Russia, however, were still a cause for concern for Bismarck. When the Russians tried to secure a loan from German banks Bismarck used his influence to block the transaction, with the result that the Russians turned to France for financial assistance. Bismarck also used his influence through the Triple Alliance to encourage Austria–Hungary, Italy and Great Britain to conclude the Mediterranean Agreements of 1887. These agreements, which aimed to maintain the existing balance of power in the Mediterranean, were anti-Russian in intention.

CONCLUSION

By 1890 Bismarck had succeeded in keeping France isolated and had kept open diplomatic relations with both Austria–Hungary and Russia. There had been no war since 1870 and the balance of power which had been established in 1871 had been preserved. In these terms Bismarck's foreign policy had been a success. He had succeeded, however, by using a series of short-term expedients to deal with the immediate problems. This was where Bismarck's skill and expertise as a diplomat and a politician were at their most effective. No long-term solutions had been found to any of the problems and the intricate series of alliances and agreements which Bismarck had created could easily unravel in the hands of less experienced diplomats.

The Bulgarian crisis 1885–6. Bulgaria again caused tensions between the powers in 1885 when a revolt against Turkish rule in Eastern Rumelia led to its reunification with Bulgaria. This raised again the fears of Britain and Austria of a 'big Bulgaria' under Russian influence. The crisis was further complicated by the attempts of the Russians to install a king of Bulgaria who would be more willing to do their bidding than the existing king. The crisis caused serious tensions between Austria-Hungary and Russia and led to the collapse of the Three Emperors' Alliance.

SUMMARY QUESTIONS

1 Why did Bismarck wish to maintain peace in Europe after 1871?

2 In what ways was the 'War in Sight' crisis a serious miscalculation by Bismarck?

3 How and why did Bismarck intervene in the Eastern crisis of 1875–8?

4 How effectively did Bismarck manage relations with Russia during the period 1879–90?

5 What factors led Bismarck to acquire an overseas empire, 1884–5? Rank the factors in order of importance and give reasons for your answer.

CHAPTER 9

The fall of Bismarck

In 1888 Bismarck was 73 years old and his long period in office, with its stresses and strains, was beginning to sap his energy. Much of the time he preferred to remain on his country estate rather than work from his office in Berlin. He had no intention of relinquishing power, however, and was still determined to pursue his policies with all the vigour that he could muster.

A NEW KAISER

In that same year the old Kaiser, Kaiser Wilhelm I, died. Wilhelm I had been content to leave the day-to-day conduct of government business in the hands of his Chancellor. He was succeeded, briefly, by his son Friedrich but within three months he too was dead from cancer. This brought the young Wilhelm II to the throne. At 29 years old, Wilhelm II was inexperienced but impatient, unstable and impetuous. A born autocrat, he was not prepared to accept the figurehead role which his grandfather had adopted. Wilhelm II was determined to be at the heart of policy making in the government of his Empire. He was also highly critical of Bismarck, and his court quickly became a magnet for the many officials and politicians who opposed the old Chancellor.

Wilhelm II.

Conflict with Bismarck

The first clash between Chancellor and Kaiser arose over Bismarck's anti-socialist campaign. Wilhelm II, at the start of his reign, was keen to present himself as a champion of the working class. In 1889 he intervened in a miners' strike in the Ruhr and lectured the employers on their social responsibilities. When Bismarck proposed to make his Anti-Socialist Law permanent, including the controversial clause which gave the police powers to expel socialist agitators, the new Kaiser opposed him. Bismarck, however, went ahead and presented the Bill to the Reichstag only to lose the vote. His political allies in the **Kartell** group of parties were split on the issue. Some Conservatives supported it but the National Liberals and Free Conservatives opposed the clause.

Bismarck's options. Bismarck decided to dissolve the Reichstag and call a general election. The results were, for him, a disaster. The Kartell parties lost seats whilst the **Radicals** and Socialists both gained, with the SPD receiving more votes than any other party. The election was a vote of no confidence in Bismarck and left him without a workable majority in the Reichstag. He now had two possible courses of action open to him. One was to forge a new Kartell made up of the Conservatives and the Centre party, an option which never had any realistic chance of success. The other was to stage a coup d'état and amend the constitution and reduce the powers of the Reichstag. Initially Wilhelm II, who was equally alarmed at the rise of the SPD, was sympathetic to this idea but he then changed his mind. Bismarck's options were running out and his authority was rapidly waning.

Bismarck's resignation

Bismarck tried to protect his authority by reviving an out-of-date Prussian Cabinet order of 1852 which required all Prussian ministers to communicate with the King only through the Minister-President. Wilhelm II demanded the withdrawal of this order or, failing that, Bismarck's resignation. There were also differences of opinion between Bismarck and Wilhelm II over foreign policy. The Kaiser complained that Bismarck had failed to keep him informed of events in Russia and he opposed Bismarck's policy of renewing the Reinsurance Treaty with Russia. It was these disagreements which Bismarck chose to make as the cause of his resignation which was offered to the Kaiser, and accepted, in March 1890. Few voices were raised in support of Bismarck and only his son resigned with him. After 28 years of being in charge of policy in Prussia and in the Reich, it was his vindictiveness and petty jealousy which was remembered by the many enemies he had made on the way, not his genius as a politician and a diplomat.

GERMANY IN 1890

The Germany of 1890 was very different from that which had existed in 1848. In the place of 39 states, loosely linked together in a German Confederation dominated by Austria, there was, in 1890, a German Reich dominated by Prussia. The economy had grown and developed and Germany was on the verge of becoming the world's second largest industrial economy. More of the German people lived in towns and cities and worked in industry. German manufacturers had established themselves as major suppliers to overseas markets. In some respects, the German political system was more advanced than most other European countries, with a Reichstag elected by universal male suffrage, and the most extensive social welfare benefits of any country.

To many observers, therefore, Germany was a modern state. Yet there were still powerful elements of the old Germany entrenched in the political and social structure of the Reich. It had a monarchical system which left ultimate power in the hands of the Kaiser. Most of the royal houses which ruled their separate states in 1848 still retained their thrones within the Reich. In Prussia, the Junker landowning aristocracy still kept their dominant position within the political system, the army and the civil service of the state. This tension between the traditional and the modern was becoming increasingly difficult to manage as Germany underwent far-reaching social and economic change.

SUMMARY QUESTIONS

1 What evidence is there that Bismarck was losing control over events 1889–90?

2 What were the issues on which Bismarck and Wilhelm II disagreed?

3 Which was the most important factor that forced Bismarck to resign?

CHAPTER 10

Germany under Wilhelm II, 1890–1914

The departure of Bismarck signalled a new era in German politics. This new era was marked by certain themes: the dominance of the Kaiser Wilhelm II and with this the central role of the army, the impact of economic and social change leading to a growth in the size and importance of the working class, and the growth of socialism. Events in domestic politics took place against the background of an arms race and increasing tension between the great powers.

KAISER WILHELM II

The period of German history between 1890 and 1914 cannot be studied without reference to the character of Wilhelm II. The Kaiser was at the heart of the German state. With Bismarck's dismissal, Wilhelm asserted more influence in domestic and foreign affairs. While taking advice from courtiers such as **Philipp von Eulenberg**, Wilhelm wielded ultimate power. The period 1890–1914 saw four chancellors in contrast to Bismarck's nineteen years in office. The significance of this fact is that the Kaiser increasingly dominated the decision-making process at the expense of the Chancellor.

The Kaiser's personality. As the Kaiser's personality dominated German political life, so the fortunes of various institutions changed. The army's influence increased considerably and by 1914 important decisions were taken by military councils rather than by civilian politicians. Equally important was Wilhelm's contempt for the Reichstag as an institution. His fear of socialism and his violent anti-Semitism were part of a deep personal insecurity. He suffered fits of rage, and hated his mother and England, the country of her birth which pointed to considerable psychological problems. The Kaiser's beliefs and personality were to have a considerable impact on Germany.

KEY PERSON

Philipp von Eulenberg For many years Philipp von Eulenberg was at the centre of court life and the favourite of Wilhelm II. On his suggestion Caprivi was removed and Hohenlohe installed as Chancellor. He was also instrumental in the rise of Bülow to Chancellor. In 1906 Philipp von Eulenberg was accused by journalist Maximilian Harden of being homosexual (homosexual activity was illegal in Wilhelmian Germany) and the accusations destroyed his credibility.

KEY QUOTE

In 1900 Friedrich Naumann wrote: 'There is no stronger force in the Germany of today than Kaiserdom'. Maximilian Harden said in 1902 that 'the Kaiser is his own Reich Chancellor. All the important political decisions of the past twelve years have been made by him'.

ECONOMIC AND SOCIAL CHANGE

New industries

From the late 1880s investment in German industry by banks grew. The result was that industry flourished. The banks were attracted to invest by the development of new industries such as chemicals and electricity. Many of Germany's leading industrialists were prepared to turn their businesses into **joint stock companies** thereby allowing investment in them from outsiders. Germany dominated many of the new industries of the time: by the 1890s Germany produced around 90 per cent of the world's dyestuffs and dominated drugs manufacture. Germany also led the world in the production of a variety of chemicals which were useful in the production of fertilisers: the production of ammonia rose by around 350 per cent between 1897 and 1907 to 287,000 tons per year. Germany had an abundance of coal and potash, the raw materials that made such an expansion in the chemicals industry possible.

Technical education. The production of chemicals demanded a high degree of specialisation which the Germans were able to provide. This was because of the high quality of their technical education system. By 1914 Germany had 58,000 full-time technical students whereas Britain had around one-sixth of that number. In 1899 German technical schools were given equal status with universities. Also significant was the fact that large German companies invested heavily in training. In 1900 the company **BASF** employed 6300 workers and 165 chemists. Such a ratio of workers to researchers was not to be found elsewhere in Europe. In 1907 over 77 per cent of managers in German industry had higher education experience. It was not just in the new industries that the German education system was superior. By 1910 there were 20 agricultural schools in Germany spreading information about new farming techniques.

The creation of cartels. The process of investment in business was not without risk. To reduce that risk investors encouraged the creation of **cartels** which would reduce competition and fix prices and production levels. All major

German and British industrial production, 1870–1910

thousand metric tons	1870	1890	1910
Coal	UK 110,000	UK 184,000	UK 268,000
	Germany 37,000	Germany 89,000	Germany 192,000
Pig iron	UK 6060	UK 8033	UK 10,380
	Germany 1391	Germany 4038	Germany 14,793
Steel	UK 286	UK 3637	UK 6374
	Germany 169	Germany 2161	Germany 13,698

industries became dominated by cartels. By 1904 the Rheinish–Westphalian Coal Syndicate controlled 98 per cent of Germany's coal production; by 1905 there were 306 cartels dominating industrial production in goods from cement to chemicals. The growing economic power of the cartels was a factor that would not be ignored by the government.

Industrial production and social change

The evidence for German economic expansion can be seen in the astonishing growth in the production of raw materials and basic industrial goods. This rapid industrialisation caused significant social change. In 1882 42.5 per cent of Germans were employed in industry and trade with 42.5 per cent employed in agriculture. These figures were to alter considerably by 1907 with 56.2 per cent in industry and only 28.6 per cent in agriculture. The proportion of Germans living in cities with a population of over 100,000 grew from 4.8 per cent in 1871 to 21.3 per cent in 1911. The fastest-growing towns and cities were those such as the mining town of Gelsenkirchen in Westphalia that relied on the expanding industries of coal, iron and steel.

Migration. Of the 60 per cent of inhabitants of Gelsenkirchen who were miners in 1907 over half had migrated from the countryside. They came in search of the higher living standards created by the economic boom of the pre-war period. Income per head, for example, grew from 352 marks per year in the early 1870s to 728 marks per year in 1911–13. Emigration declined as the growth in employment opportunities was able to absorb the rapidly growing population. However, such jobs were also necessary to meet the demand for employment from those displaced by a depressed agricultural sector.

Agriculture

As with the rest of Europe, German agriculture suffered from falling prices as a result of overproduction and foreign competition. This overproduction was in part due to the growth in the mechanisation of agriculture, for example the introduction of threshing machines to over 1 million holdings between 1882 and 1907. However, mechanisation was labour saving and created unemployment. The demands for protection against American grain reached a crescendo by the turn of the century and the agrarian-based political lobby became an ever-increasing pressure group in Wilhelmian Germany. Even though the numbers of those employed in agriculture dropped considerably, still 40 per cent of the population were based in the countryside. In particular the *Mittelstand* formed the bedrock of the agrarian community. Although yields increased and 4 million acres were newly cultivated in the period 1880–1900, the agricultural community felt threatened by the increasing influence of industry. On occasions, such as in 1902 when Bülow increased tariffs, there was an 'alliance of steel and rye' (manufacturing and agrarian interests).

THE GROWTH OF SOCIALISM, 1890–1905

Linked closely to rapid industrialisation and urbanisation was the growth in the size and importance of the socialist movement. After the dismissal of Bismarck his Anti-Socialist Law was allowed to lapse which gave a significant boost to the movement. In the election to the Reichstag in 1890 the socialist SPD won nearly 1.5 million votes and 35 seats. However, the party was split between those who accepted parliamentary democracy as the means to achieve

KEY THEME

The Erfurt Programme was written by Kautsky in 1891. In it he explained his belief in passive radicalism.

KEY PERSON

Karl Kautsky was seen as the expert on Marxist theory in the socialist movement. He believed that capitalism was on the verge of collapse so the socialists should simply concentrate on achieving a majority in the Reichstag.

KEY PERSON

Eduard Bernstein In the 1880s Bernstein was the chief editor of the party newspaper, the *Social Democrat*. He emigrated to England in the 1880s and maintained close links with the Fabian movement. He was a close friend of leading socialist thinker Friedrich Engels and it was not until after Engels' death in 1895 that he began to develop his theories of revisionism.

KEY STATISTICS

The rise in the seats won by the SPD in Reichstag elections, 1890–1912

1890	35
1893	44
1898	56
1903	81
1907	43
1912	110

social reform (the revisionists) and those such as August Bebel who argued that revolutionary means were the socialists' only real alternative. The **Erfurt Programme** of 1891 affirmed the doctrine of the SPD as being Marxist. To **Karl Kautsky**, who drew up the Erfurt Programme, the collapse of the capitalist system was inevitable according to the so-called 'catastrophe theory'. Therefore, there was no need for violent revolution but neither should the SPD involve itself in middle-class politics.

Socialist revisionism

Such views were challenged by revisionists within the party. In 1891 the leader of the SPD in Bavaria, George von Vollmar outlined the view that advancement could be made within the political system. The contrast between Vollmar's and Kautsky's views reflected ideological and regional variations in the ranks of the SPD, southern socialists being primarily reformists. In 1894 Vollmar put his views into practice by voting in favour of the Bavarian state budget because it contained provision for social reforms. His views were backed up by the writer **Eduard Bernstein** who argued that socialism could be best achieved through parliamentary means and in alliance with the middle class. At the Hanover conference in 1899 Bernstein's views were condemned but they had gained acceptance among many within the party ranks.

The significance of the trade union movement in the growth of socialism

The cause of reformism was most importantly put forward by the leadership of the trade union movement. The power of the union movement was considerable. In 1890 a new central organisation was formed, the General Commission of Trades Unions. Led by **Carl Legien** it rejected the revolutionary stance of the SPD and argued in favour of political representation as the means by which workers could improve their standard of living and conditions of work. The battle between party and unions came to a head at the Trade Union Congress in Cologne in 1905 and Mannheim in 1906.

Although the socialist movement was gradually moving towards a more reformist approach, Germany's rulers continued to behave as if the SPD represented a serious threat to the foundations of the Reich. The four Chancellors who directed German affairs between 1890 and 1914 did not, however, follow a consistent policy towards the socialists.

THE CHANCELLORSHIP OF LEO VON CAPRIVI, 1890–4

The dismissal of Bismarck in 1890 did little to resolve some of the problems of German politics. The new Chancellor General Leo von Caprivi was given the task of undertaking social reforms that would distract the working class from socialism and reduce social tension. Caprivi attempted to reform with these aims in mind.

- Industrial courts were set up in July 1890 to adjudicate in wage disputes and restrict hours of work for women.
- Workers were given the right to form committees.
- Protection of agriculture was reduced by a reduction on duties on imported wheat and rye, and of tariffs on imported German manufactured goods. This was to lay the basis for the expansion of German trade. It was also hoped that the reduction in duties would appeal to the working class by provoking a fall in food prices.

Reaction against Caprivi

The reforms of Caprivi were not to have the desired effects. The reaction of the grain producers was one of bitterness and frustration which resulted in the formation in 1893 of the Agrarian League (*Bund der Landwirte*). The support for the League reflected the tensions between industrial and agricultural interests; within a year it had a membership of 250,000 members. The League was to form the basis of the conservative movement for the years that followed.

KEY PERSON

Carl Legien worked hard to promote reformism. As leader of the General Commission he co-operated with employers over the introduction of wage scales and the co-operation of workers with the state. Legien was to survive the First World War and took an active part in opposing the Kapp Putsch (an attempt by the monarchist Wolfgang Kapp to seize power) in Germany in 1920.

Caprivi managed to alienate other groups through political mismanagement and miscalculation.

Minister-President of Prussia This was a particularly important position. Control of the Prussian government was vital to avoid a situation of dual power developing. Caprivi's resignation did just that and his successor as Minister-President of Prussia Count Eulenberg became a powerful critic.

- **Prussian School Bill, 1892.** As part of the Kulturkampf Bismarck had confiscated Church monies and had restricted the Church's role in education. In attempting to appease the Centre party, Caprivi encouraged the Prussian Minister of Education to propose a Prussian School Bill which would restore some of the Church's privileges. Such was the opposition to these plans from National Liberals, many Conservatives and even socialists that Caprivi backed down but not before he had managed to alienate a wide cross-section of the political establishment. As a result Caprivi was forced to resign as Minister-President of Prussia.
- **Army Bill, 1892/3.** In June 1890 the German government led by Caprivi allowed the Reinsurance Treaty with Russia to lapse. The resulting agreement between France and Russia made the military leadership led by Chief of Staff Count von Schlieffen nervous of encirclement. Von Schlieffen called for an increase in the size of the army reserve. Caprivi agreed but recognised that it would be difficult to get the Reichstag to agree to the increase in expenditure needed to strengthen the army by up to 84,000 men. As a bargaining tool he offered a reduction in service from three to two years for conscripts and an agreement that the Reichstag could discuss the military budget every five instead of seven years.

Camarilla The term applied to the group of favourites that surrounded Wilhelm II.

Despite having the Kaiser's backing for such plans the concessions made by Caprivi upset the nationalist right. The Bill was passed into law only after an election in 1893 in which the number of Progressives in the Reichstag was significantly reduced (66 to 37) and Caprivi had made further concessions on the numbers of recruits to be drafted. Caprivi had fallen foul of the **Camarilla** that surrounded Wilhelm and he resigned in October 1894. It might well be argued that Caprivi managed to provoke greater political opposition in his attempts to deal with economic and diplomatic change.

CHANCELLORSHIP OF PRINCE ZU HOHENLOHE-SCHILLINGSFÜRST, 1894–1900

Hohenlohe was chosen as Chancellor because he posed no political threat to those who surrounded the Kaiser. The period of his Chancellorship was marked by an increasingly bitter attitude of the Kaiser and his entourage against the socialists and the working-class movement.

- In 1895 an Anti-Subversion Bill was thrown out by the Reichstag. This was also the fate of the Bill of August 1899 inspired by the Kaiser to imprison strikers who threatened the security of the state.
- The Kaiser objected to what he saw as an encroachment on his prerogative by the successful attempt by the Reichstag in 1898 to reform the Prussian military justice system. Not only that but in 1897 the Reichstag had forced a cut of 12 million Reichsmarks on the naval estimates.

Such defeat was due to the fact that the alliance of Conservatives, Free Conservatives and National Liberals did not have a majority in the Reichstag.

Navy Law and Flottenpolitik

Despite defeat in 1897 the first Navy Law was passed in 1898 as public sentiment swayed the Centre party into voting for a vast increase in naval subsidies. Although very much associated with **Admiral von Tirpitz**, the Navy Law was promoted by a Kaiser who was very much at the heart of the military planning process. He had accepted von Tirpitz's **Risk Theory** that, by building such a fleet, Britain would be forced to seek a treaty with Germany.

Weltpolitik and Flottenpolitik

The Kaiser ignored Hohenlohe's opinions (calling him a 'straw doll' Chancellor) and undermined him by removing his key ministers in 1896 and in the summer of 1897 – a step crucial to the political development of Wilhelmian Germany. Not only did it see installed von Bülow as Foreign Secretary and von Tirpitz as Secretary of state at

KEY TERM

Navy League Set up by the Reich Navy Office and funded by industrialists, who hoped to benefit from a programme of shipbuilding, the Navy League had a membership of 270,000 by 1900.

the Naval Office but it also heralded a new set of policies including *Weltpolitik* and *Flottenpolitik*. The aim behind these policies was clear. The Kaiser hoped that militarist policies would raise support for the monarchy and military as opposed to the Reichstag. Support for a more aggressive imperial policy was organised by groups including the Colonial League and the **Navy League**. The policy of *Weltpolitik* was primarily aimed at imperial expansion and military dominance. It was to have important consequences diplomatically, seeing the destruction of Bismarck's system, and allowing the Kaiser to take a more interfering role in decision-making.

CHANCELLORSHIP OF COUNT BERNARD VON BÜLOW, 1900–9

There is no doubt that von Bülow had been groomed as Hohenlohe's replacement by Wilhelm's inner circle of courtiers especially Philipp von Eulenberg. He was also a favourite of Wilhelm. However, he did not follow the example of his predecessor who placed repressive legislation before the Reichstag. Instead, he followed a more conciliatory line in domestic affairs. In particular, he accepted the tactic first suggested by **Johannes Miquel** in 1897 of *Sammlungspolitik.* This was a coming together of the productive classes of manufacturer and landowner to defeat the common enemy of socialism. There were two main aspects of this policy.

KEY PERSON

Johannes Miquel was the Deputy Prime Minister of Prussia. In 1897 he clearly stated his rationale for *Sammlungspolitik* as: 'The great task of the present is without prejudice to gather together all the elements which support the state and thereby to prepare for the unavoidable battle against the Social Democratic movement'.

- **Navy Law.** In 1900 a second Navy Law was passed which provided for a seventeen-year building programme and the construction of a high seas fleet that would be second only to the Royal Navy.
- **Protectionism.** In 1902 von Bülow reversed the tariff concessions arranged by Caprivi. The new Tariff Law restored the high duties on agricultural products and reflected the power of the Agrarian League. Most importantly for agricultural interests, the tariffs on Russian grain that had been reduced in 1894 were restored.

Opposition to Bülow. The tariff reforms had been introduced to please the Conservative block inside and outside the Reichstag. However, the new Tariff Law was highly unpopular in the country because it was widely believed that it would increase the price of foodstuffs. In the 1903 elections to the Reichstag the SPD won 25 more seats than in the 1898 election. The following three years saw Bülow struggle to hold together a coalition government made up of Conservatives, National Liberals and the Centre party. The naval building programme and an active foreign policy stretched government finances but any attempts at taxation reform were blocked by agrarian interests. The Centre party used its position in the coalition to follow an independent line. In 1905 it joined with the socialists in the Reichstag in voting against an increase in expenditure on the cavalry. It also defeated a Bill for the reorganisation of the Colonial Office and it refused funds for military operations against an uprising in German South West Africa.

The 'Bülow Bloc' and the 1907 election

Bülow used the criticism of the socialists, Catholics and others of the administration's colonial policy to good effect. In the campaign for the 1907 election Bülow painted his opponents as unpatriotic. He enticed the Progressives to join a new coalition based on support for *Weltpolitik*. This was an ingenious piece of electioneering, the **Bülow Bloc** winning a crushing electoral victory with 216 seats as opposed to the 105 seats of the Centre party. The SPD was squeezed out in an atmosphere of patriotism, losing 36 seats. However, the result of the election did not give security to Bülow's Chancellorship.

- **Centre party.** The Centre party deeply resented its treatment and became determined to oppose Bülow at every stage.
- **Tension with the Progressives.** Having brought the Progressives into the ruling coalition, Bülow now had to ensure that they stayed. However, tension arose with the Progressives' demand for a reform to the three-tier electoral system.
- **Taxation.** By 1908 the army and navy together cost a vast 1200 million Reichsmarks per year. Bülow's hands

KEY TERM

Bülow Bloc This coalition was put together with the expressed aim of excluding the Centre party. The parties that joined the coalition included the Conservatives, Free Conservatives, Agrarian League, the National Liberals and the Progressives.

Germany policy during the Boer war Throughout the Boer war German public opinion had sided with the Boers. Before the outbreak of war the Kaiser had infuriated British public opinion by sending a telegram to President Kruger of the South African Republic congratulating him on the defeat of a British attack on his territory known as the Jameson Raid.

The relationship between the Kaiser and von Bülow In 1897 von Bülow was appointed Foreign Secretary by the Kaiser. On his appointment the Kaiser announced: 'Bülow will be my Bismarck and just as he hammered Germany together externally with Grand Papa's help, so shall we two clean up the rubbish heap of parliamentarianism and the party system at home.' Despite being initially slavish in his admiration for the Kaiser, von Bülow became increasingly exasperated with his leader's political conduct.

were tied in that the Conservatives and Agrarian League opposed an increase in taxation to deal with the mounting financial crisis. However the Progressives believed that the only way to resolve the financial situation was by increasing property taxes. In order to create disharmony in the ranks of the coalition, the Centre party supported the Conservatives.

The Daily Telegraph Affair

Bülow's undoing was his handling of the storm of protest which greeted the publication in 1908 of an interview with Wilhelm in the British newspaper the *Daily Telegraph*. In the interview Wilhelm gave himself the credit for **a pro-British policy during the Boer war**. The Kaiser also seemed to suggest that, while he himself was pro-British, German public opinion was not. Bülow had been given a transcript of the interview before its publication but had not read it. In the Reichstag he attempted to cover his own negligence while only half-heartedly defending the Kaiser's actions. Despite its fury the Reichstag failed to act to limit the powers of the monarchy. **Bülow had lost the confidence of the Kaiser** and resigned in July 1909.

THE CHANCELLORSHIP OF VON BETHMANN HOLLWEG, 1909–17

The resignation of Bülow and the appointment of Bethmann Hollweg exemplified the authority of the Kaiser. Hollweg's strengths did not lie in foreign policy and his appointment left the Kaiser to take the initiative in that area. He was limited in his actions by the continuing budget crisis and conservative opposition to reform.

Reform of the Prussian Parliament

The most divisive political issue in Germany was that of constitutional reform. Whereas the Reichstag was elected on a one-person-one-vote system, in Prussia the lower house of Parliament was elected on a three-class system. Essentially this meant that the votes of the middle and lower classes were worth less than those of the upper class. The result was conservative control of the Prussian Parliament and also the civil service. In 1910 Hollweg

decided to introduce reform to the **Prussian electoral system** as the means by which socialist agitation could be reduced. His plans were received with such hostility that they were dropped. He also faced a severe budget crisis made worse by his efforts to increase the size of the army.

Military expansion

Army Bill, 1912. In response to growing international tension, support grew for expansion of the German army to enable it to implement the **Schlieffen Plan** and deal with a potential war on two fronts. The bill increased the strength of the army by some 29,000 men.

Army Bill, 1913. All previous Army Bills were eclipsed by the Army Bill of 1913. Given the levels of military and diplomatic tension in Europe, the Chief of Staff Molkte was able to persuade Hollweg to agree to an increase in the army's size from 544,000 to 870,000. The Army Bill passed the Reichstag in June 1913 despite the opposition of the Socialists. It was to have important repercussions. The cost of the new measure was estimated to have been

---

KEY THEME

The Prussian electoral system The anomalies produced by the electoral system were clear. In the 1908 election for the Prussian lower house of Parliament the Socialist candidates received 23 per cent of the vote but gained only seven seats. The Conservatives received 16 per cent of the vote but gained 212 seats. Despite demonstrations and the attempts of Socialists in the Reichstag to alter the system there was no change.

KEY TERM

Schlieffen Plan The Chief of the General Staff Count Alfred Schlieffen drew up the plan in 1902. The plan was the military's response to the possibility of war on two fronts. Schlieffen planned for a quick war in the west against France to be followed by war against Russia.

435 million Reichsmarks for 1913 alone. In order to finance this measure, Hollweg was obliged to raise a special defence tax on property. The Socialists voted for the tax, not to support militarism but out of a desire to assert the principle of direct taxation on property.

By 1912 there was a sense of crisis at the heart of government in the Reich, largely because of:

- the continued growth of the SPD which had become the largest party in the Reichstag in 1912
- continuing conflict between Reichstag and government in which the Chancellor could not guarantee majorities for his policies and the Reichstag could not make the government accountable
- the fragmentation of right-wing politics.

The 1912 elections to the Reichstag
In 1910 the many different radical groups came together to form the **Fortschrittliche Vereinigung**. Their support for the SPD in the second ballot of the 1912 election was to be crucial. Meanwhile Hollweg had refused to adopt a nationalist stance, as had Bülow in 1907, and high food prices gave the Socialists the opportunity to campaign against protectionism. The election result was a sensation. The Socialists won 67 new seats which gave them 110 deputies and made them the largest party in the Reichstag. However, victory did not bring the Socialists any closer to power. Indeed their victory in 1912 reflects the limitations of Reichstag power. Many Socialists would not entertain a coalition with middle-class parties but there were few among left-leaning liberals who would support the Socialists. Most parties in the Reichstag represented sectional interest groups. This made coalitions difficult as was discovered after 1918. The election was a staggering defeat for the conservative elites.

Zabern Affair, 1913
The increasing influence of the military on domestic affairs in Germany on the eve of war can best be seen in the events of the Zabern Affair. The tension between German military forces stationed in the provinces and local citizens was high. In 1913 a lieutenant of the German army

KEY TERM

The Fortschrittliche Vereinigung was formed in order to reverse the decline in German liberalism. It had 120,000 members by 1912. However, it tended not to attract the support of the working class. Therefore, to wield influence it joined in alliance with the Socialists.

KEY QUOTE

Heinrich Class, the leader of the **Pan-German League**, said in 1912 that 'the propertied classes, the pillars of our national economy, see themselves exposed to the arbitrary power of the working class, spurred on by socialism'.

KEY TERM

Pan-German League The aims of the Pan-German League were to promote German nationalism and establish a greater Germany which would see the unity of the German-speaking peoples. The League was founded in the 1890s and was the most extreme Pan-German organisation. It was violently anti-Semitic and preached racial hatred. At its peak it had only 20,000 members.

stationed in Zabern in Alsace made damning remarks about the quality of the young Alsatian recruits. Demonstrations followed and the local commanding officer Colonel von Reuter ordered the streets to be cleared. The Reichstag was indignant at the actions of the military and Hollweg was not willing to side with the politicians against the army. On 4 December 1913 the Reichstag passed a vote of no-confidence against him by 293 votes to 54. Hollweg survived because the constitution was clear that he was responsible to the Kaiser, not the Reichstag. The Zabern Affair highlighted the influence of the army and conservative groups in Wilhelmian Germany. It also underlined the weakness of the Reichstag.

The radicalisation of right-wing politics

Between the 1890s and the beginning of the First World War important changes were taking place in middle-class Germany. The creation of sectional interest groups should be seen as a direct result of the economic changes of the period. The rise of the organised right had as great an impact on German politics as the rise in importance of the socialist movement. As important as the *Sammlungspolitik* (see page 97), was the organisation of different sectional groups to protect their interests against the impact of economic modernisation and falling agricultural prices.

Agrarian groups. The Agrarian League, founded in 1893, became politically most important. In the elections in 1898 the National Liberals survived politically in the countryside by committing themselves to the programme of the Agrarian League and protection.

Middle-class groups. There was no one group that represented the *Mittelstand* and its political priorities until the founding of the Mittelstand Association in 1904 and the Mittelstand League in 1911. The lower middle class was organised into a range of groups from the socialist Association of Commercial Assistants on the left to the right-wing German-national Commercial Assistants' Association.

Nationalist groups. These were formed with the intention of lobbying in favour of national priorities. They were not politically neutral or objective but campaigned from an often-aggressive anti-socialist viewpoint. There was a range of such organisations from the Pan-German League founded in 1891 to the Imperial League Against Social Democracy founded in 1904 and the Defence League of 1912. The importance of these groups was that they helped to radicalise German politics.

Anti-Semitism. The violent anti-Semitic views held by Wilhelm II were also held by many of his subjects. At the Tivoli Conference in 1892 the Conservative party adopted anti-Semitism as part of its political manifesto. They demanded the exclusion of Jews from the civil service and posts of importance in the army. In the Reichstag election in 1893, anti-Semitic parties such as the *Reformpartei* won 15 seats. Although they did not influence legislation, the existence of such parties reflected the depth of anti-Semitic feeling in Germany.

CONCLUSION: HOW WAS POLICY MADE IN WILHELM'S GERMANY?

Impact of foreign policy on domestic affairs

There is a clear link between German foreign policy and the course of internal politics between 1890–1914. The historical debate revolves around the extent of that link.

The main argument is that foreign policy was used as a means of manipulating public opinion. The clearest example of this was von Bülow's campaign in the 1907 election based on nationalist and imperialist slogans. The reason for such a policy was to keep the socialist threat at bay and heal the deep political and social divisions that had emerged out of the unification process and economic change.

The Berghahn thesis. The historian V.R. Berghahn has argued that Germany's foreign policy was very much dictated by the effects of rapid industrialisation. According to Berghahn internal pressures were at least as important as diplomatic pressures in pushing Germany's leaders to war. The economy was seriously overburdened by the expansion of army and navy which made an aggressive foreign policy more likely as a justification for such expenditure. There is no doubt that after 1890 the Kaiser and his circle took a more aggressive stance against the Reichstag. The fear as shown in the promotion of *Sammlungspolitik* did not just stem from socialism but also from the hostility to any extension in the influence of the Reichstag.

Weltpolitik. *Weltpolitik* and the introduction of the first Navy Law in 1897 were a watershed in foreign policy. Tirpitz himself recognised the impact that building a fleet would have on domestic affairs. Not only did he hope to build a fleet to challenge Britain's fleet but also he wished to create a navy which could act as a focal point for the nation. In fact, *Weltpolitik* acted to encourage a form of nationalism that was divisive rather than healing.

The role of Kaiser Wilhelm II. There have been surprisingly few attempts to interpret the role of the Kaiser. One argument suggests that the dismissal of Bismarck left a power vacuum that was not filled by the Kaiser, and that the post-Bismarck Germany was in a state of permanent crisis. Power was held by those at court who surrounded the Kaiser, such as Philipp von Eulenberg, and the industrial and political élites. Wilhelm and his succession of ministers resorted to repression as the means by which they governed and to political manipulation of the German people through the Navy League and other organisations. This view is contradicted by the evidence which emerges from the private papers of the Grand Duke Friedrich I of Baden: these show that the Kaiser took a central role in the decision-making process of the Reich.

There has been some debate between historians as to whether the period could be described as one of 'personal rule'. Erich Eyck argued that Wilhelm did have personal rule but this view has been countered by Fritz Hartung and Ernst Rudolf who argued that Wilhelm was constrained by the constitution. John Röhl has tried to qualify the arguments of both. Röhl points out that the Kaiser's rule was not constant, that the period 1890–7 was more of a period of personal rule than the time during the Chancellorship of von Bülow when the Kaiser interfered

KEY THEME

War council of 1912
Admiral von Müller describes the council in his diaries. It was attended by the Kaiser and other leading military figures who made plans to go to war. The discussion at the council revolved around the timing of war, Tirpitz arguing for a 'postponement of the great fight for one and a half years'. The discussions of the 'war council' showed all the insecurities of the Wilhelmian establishment: British naval superiority, the spread of Pan-Slavism in the Balkans, and the menace of democracy and socialism at home.

KEY THEME

Bethmann Hollweg's memorandum In the memorandum Bethmann defined Germany's war aims as: 'The security of the German Empire in the West and in the East for the foreseeable future. To this end, France must be so weakened that she cannot rise again as a great power, Russia must be pushed as far as possible from the German frontier, and her rule over non-Russian subject peoples must be broken.'

KEY QUOTE

The Kaiser's response to the assassination of Franz Ferdinand was most telling: 'Now or never. The Serbs will have to be straightened out and soon.'

less in the affairs of state. The historian Isabel Hull has shown that the Kaiser was at the centre of an extensive administrative organisation. He was also at the centre of a wide group of admirers at court and beyond, including the Liebenberg group. The important point is that these powerful personalities who dominated the structures of Wilhelmian Germany did so with Wilhelm's blessing and at his choice.

Given the evidence that Wilhelm had a central role in policy by the turn of the century, it is appropriate to argue that he was more than a 'shadow chancellor'. While Bismarck's legacy, immature relations with the Reichstag and Wilhelm's personal insecurities might have overshadowed the first ten years of his reign, it is clear that by the turn of the century he was the important decision maker. The Navy Bills of 1897 and 1900 that put Germany on a collision course with Britain were of his prompting. By 1900 the Kaiser had full control over the decision-making of his ministers. This was to have a significant effect, as revealed in a **'war council'** held in 1912. From 1911 to 1914 Hollweg reacted to the desires of his master rather than seek a diplomatic solution to the rising tension. Indeed, the Chancellor shared many of the aims of the military establishment as is revealed in his **memorandum** of September 1914.

Decision for war. After the assassination of Franz Ferdinand in June 1914, the Kaiser gave the Austro-Hungarian Foreign Minister what became known as 'the Blank Cheque'. This amounted to unconditional support from Germany to the Austrians in dealing with the Serbs as they saw fit. In Germany the decision to mobilise in support of the Austrians was taken ultimately by the Kaiser in consultation with his generals. The role of Bethmann in the drift to war is debatable. However, it was clear that he did not attempt to look for a diplomatic settlement and it is highly unlikely that the decision for war was in Hollweg's hands. His choices became further narrowed by events which followed. The mobilisation of Austro-Hungarian forces on 30 July provoked the order for mobilisation in Russia the next day. Russian mobilisation played into the hands of the German government, as anti-

Russian sentiment soon put paid to any SPD-organised anti-war demonstration. On 1 August Germany declared war against Russia and mobilised.

Conclusion

On the eve of the Great War, Germany was a country with severe internal difficulties. The country was run by a conservative, landowning élite who resisted all demands for reform. Their power was entrenched in the government of Prussia, the civil service, the army and in the monarchy. Despite the fact that anti-government parties had achieved a majority in the Reichstag elections of 1912, these forces had minimal influence over government policy. At the pinnacle of this system stood Wilhelm II, whose mental instability had had damaging consequences for policy-making. Equally damaging was the fact that Wilhelm increasingly surrounded himself with military men and listened to their advice more than to that of his civilian ministers, some of whom believed that a victorious war would be the way to solve Germany's internal problems.

There was, however, another side to this story. Although there were strikes over issues like wages, political protests were rare. The majority of the people had benefited from increased living standards as a result of industrial expansion. Despite the government's difficulties in achieving Reichstag majorities, the Reich never came under any serious threats from its opponents. This was partly due to the success of the aristocratic landowners in forging a partnership with the industrialists – 'the alliance of steel and rye' – and partly due to the timidity of the parliamentary opposition. In August 1914, even the supposedly anti-war socialists were prepared to vote for the war credits which the government needed to pay for the war. Germany entered the war with the ruling élite still very much in control and with a greater degree of political consensus than at any time since 1871.

AS ASSESSMENT: GERMANY 1848–1914

STRUCTURED QUESTIONS IN THE STYLE OF OCR

In the period 1862–71 Germany was united under Prussian domination. The following factors helped to make this possible:

a) economic developments, including the Zollverein
b) the role of Bismarck
c) Prussian military victories
d) the growth of German nationalism.

1 Choose TWO of these factors and explain their contributions to the success of Prussia.

2 Compare the importance of THREE of these factors in the process of German unification.

Reading
Before answering these questions you should read Chapters 1, 2, 3 and 4 of the AS part of this book. You will also find it useful to refer to Section 2 of the A2 part.

Planning
Plan your answers before you begin. In your plans you need to identify the key points you wish to make and how they relate to the question. Every question contains key words which you need to identify and use as the focus of your answer. In Question 1 the key words are 'explain', 'contributions' and 'success'. In Question 2 they are 'compare', 'importance' and 'process'.

You need not give exactly equal amounts of time to the factors that you choose to write about but you must be able to demonstrate sound knowledge and understanding of each of the factors chosen. Use the mark allocation for each part of a structured question on the exam paper as a rough guide to the amount of time you should devote to it.

Writing

- Make sure your answers are focused directly on the questions. Key words are useful here.
- Your answers must have carefully selected factual examples given as supporting evidence to illustrate the points you are making in your arguments.
- Your arguments must be coherent. They must follow logically from one point to another.
- Good grammar and spelling are important.

How to answer the questions

Question 1

This question is asking you to demonstrate your knowledge and understanding of the process of German unification and the part played by a range of different factors. Although the focus of your answers will be on the years 1862–71 you will need to place the factors in a wider context. For example, if you choose to write about economic factors you will need to include the development of the Zollverein from the 1830s, the growth of railways since the 1830s and the development of Prussian industry from at least as far back as the 1850s. If you choose the growth of German nationalism as one of your factors, you should refer to the events of 1848 and the establishment of the Nationalverein in 1859.

Question 2

- This question requires a broader range of knowledge and greater depth of understanding than Question 1. You are given the option of limiting your answer to three factors or of covering all four. The factors which you have not already written about in Question 1 will need more background explanation than those you have already covered.
- The question demands a comparison. Writing about the various factors separately with very little effort to make comparisons will not gain very high marks. The more you compare the relative importance of the factors, the higher the mark you will achieve. One possible approach is to rank the factors in order of importance, carefully explaining the reasoning behind your choice. For example, if you choose to argue that the role of Bismarck was the most important factor you must not only explain what he did but also why his actions were crucial to the success of Prussia at critical moments in the process.
- The best answers will explain the links between the factors and the ways in which they were interdependent. For example, Prussia's military victories were made possible by the economic strength of Prussia relative to the other states and by the favourable diplomatic context established by Bismarck.

STRUCTURED, SOURCE-BASED QUESTIONS IN THE STYLE OF EDEXCEL

Source A

Prussia was and is dominated by a political orientation that could not and cannot lead to German unity. If this policy, which has found its archetype in Count Bismarck, conquered Germany tomorrow and unified it by force, then even this conquest of all Germany would not lead to German unity. A conquest of Germany by a Prussia that is not ruled in a German spirit would be merely a bare fact that would last until it was superseded by another fact. The unity of Germany must be founded on something beyond the 'majestic thundering of cannon' . . . it must be rooted in German respect for law, German popular honour and popular self-government if it is to last . . . The unity of Germany can be realised only by and with the German people, not by a 'Crown' with the help of a party that scorns German law and German nationality.

Jacob Venedy, a liberal politician from Cologne, writing in 1864.

Study the source and then answer the questions below:

1 In what ways does the author criticise Bismarck's methods of unifying Germany?

2 How did Bismarck ensure that Austria would be isolated during the Austro-Prussian war?

3 Why were the southern states not included in a united Germany in 1866 and then included in the Reich in 1871?

Reading

Before answering these questions you should read Chapter 4 of the AS part of this book. You would also find it useful to read Section 2 of the A2 part.

How to answer these questions
Question 1

- As a source-based question this requires careful reading of the source: you need to identify the key phrases in which the author expresses his criticism of Bismarck's methods. It is also important to place the source in its historical context and to do this you need to draw upon your background knowledge.
- The question can be answered on a number of levels. At a basic level you must demonstrate, through careful selection and quoting of key phrases, that you understand the author's main criticism of Bismarck's methods, namely that he opposes the use of force.

- To gain higher marks you will need to focus on the author's own view of how unity should be achieved and on what basis. For this, you will need to examine what he means by 'respect for law', 'popular honour' and 'popular self-government'. How do these concepts differ from Bismarck's aims and methods?
- The highest marks will go to those students who make inferences from the author's background. How did the fact that he was a liberal politician affect his attitude to unification in general and to Bismarck's methods in particular?

Question 2

This question is testing your knowledge and understanding of the events in the years 1864–6 leading to the Austro-Prussian war and of Bismarck's role in ensuring that Austria entered the war without allies. In your answer you must include the key events, particularly the Convention of Gastein and Bismarck's meeting with Napoleon at Biarritz. These events will need to be set in a wider context, such as Austria's relations with other powers at that time. Some reference to the debate over whether Bismarck was controlling events or merely taking advantage of opportunities which presented themselves to him will help you to reach the higher marks.

Question 3

This question is testing your understanding of how the position of the southern states changed between 1866 and 1871. There will need to be some comparison between the situations at the beginning and end of the period. The main focus of your answer needs to be on the factors which prevented the inclusion of the southern states in 1866 (for example, southern particularism, French opposition) and those which promoted their inclusion by 1871 (for example, military treaties with Prussia, the experience of co-operating with Prussia during the Franco-Prussian war). The better answers will differentiate between internal and external factors and between long-term and short-term factors. All answers will need to highlight the importance of the Franco-Prussian war in changing the external situation and in changing the attitudes of the southern states towards unity.

STRUCTURED SOURCE-BASED QUESTIONS IN THE STYLE OF AQA

Example A

Read the following source and then answer the questions relating to it.

> After the crucial events of 1878–9, Bismarck maintained complete conservative dominance in Germany, supported by the *alliance of 'Steel and Rye'*, and able virtually to ignore the opposition from Liberals, Catholics and Socialists.
>
> Norman Stone, *Europe Transformed, 1878–1919*, 1985.

1 Explain the meaning of the term 'alliance of Steel and Rye'.

2 Explain why the events of 1878–9 marked an important turning point in the political development of the German Reich.

3 What were the internal strengths and weaknesses of the German Reich at the time of the fall of Bismarck in 1890?

Reading
In order to answer these questions you will need to read Chapter 5 of this book. You will also find it useful to consult Chapters 6, 7 and 9 and Sections 3 and 5 of the A2 section.

How to answer the questions
Question 1
- Note that this question will be worth a few marks and does not therefore require a long answer.
- A basic, accurate definition of the term is required but in itself is not enough to earn higher marks.
- You need to put the phrase into context by explaining the rise of the industrialists because of the industrial revolution and the common interest they shared with Junker landowners over tariff reform.
- It would be useful to refer to the development of a conservative 'bloc' in German politics in the 1880s which was united in opposition to socialism.

Question 2
- This is a very big question but you cannot afford to spend too long in answering it because most of the marks are reserved for question 3. An answer of about one page in length would be appropriate.
- An explanation of a turning point requires some comparison between the situations before and after the event.
- There are three main factors which need to be included in this answer: the return to trade protection, the ending of the Kulturkampf and the introduction of the Anti-Socialist Law.
- Try to make links between these factors and to evaluate their relative significance. A key point here is that the events of 1878–9 mark the end of Bismarck's dependence on the alliance with the Liberals and the start of a more conservative phase in the politics of the Reich.

Question 3

- This question carries a high proportion of the total marks. It requires a short essay-type answer.
- There were a number of strengths and weaknesses in the Reich by 1890. Try to cover a wide range in your answer. You must also, as the question demands, cover both strengths and weaknesses.
- Try to identify any links between strengths and weaknesses and emphasise these in your answer. For example, economic growth was a strength but the resulting social change, putting strain on an outdated political system, was a weakness.
- Try to draw conclusions about Bismarck's legacy to his successors. In particular, you should focus on Bismarck's problems in managing the Reichstag and his lack of any long-term solutions to these problems.

Example B

Read the following source and answer the questions.

> The most dramatic illustration of the growth of military influence in Germany and the Chancellor's surrender to it came in November 1913 in the Alsatian town of Zabern. Army officers overstepped their authority and made wholesale arrests of civilians. Wilhelm decided that the incident at Zabern was a matter to be dealt with by his commanders and himself without civilian influence. When news of the arrests appeared in the press, there was an outcry of protest that soon exceeded in violence that aroused by the *Daily Telegraph* interview.
>
> Adapted from G.A. Craig, *Germany 1866–1945* (1981).

1 Explain the meaning of 'the Daily Telegraph interview' in the context of 1908–9?

2 How far did the events of 1907–13 challenge the dominance of the Kaiser and the ruling elites?

3 How important was the Kaiser's personality in widening political and social divisions in Germany in the period 1890–1914?

Reading

In order to answer these questions you will need to read Chapter 10 of this book.

How to answer the questions
Question 1

The question wants you to focus your answer on the *Daily Telegraph* interview and its impact on German politics. You should try to do the following in your answer:

- Explain how the Kaiser provoked opposition at home by damaging relations with Britain and how the affair led to von Bülow's dismissal.
- Place the affair in the context of Wilhelm's style of leadership, how the affair showed his contempt for public opinion and his retreat from reality.

Style

You need to answer the question directly. Here is an example of a sentence showing how you might do that:

The Daily Telegraph interview provoked a storm of protest in Germany and damaged relations with Britain. It brought to a head the growing mistrust between the Kaiser and von Bülow who only half-heartedly defended the Kaiser in the Reichstag. It also revealed the balance of power between Kaiser and Chancellor, von Bülow being dismissed soon after.

Question 2

Although there is a source at the start of the exercise, the question does not ask you to use it if you do not want to. Instead the source can act as a stimulus although it can give you a clue to at least a part of your answer. In this case it mentions the storm of protest.

The question here wants you to explain the challenges to the Kaiser. To reach the top level you should prioritise the factors you give. Below are examples of what you might include in your answer:

- The Daily Telegraph Affair, 1908
- The Eulenberg Affair, 1906
- The sacking of von Bülow
- The military budgets
- The 1912 election
- The Zabern Affair, 1913.

Plan

Before you start you should briefly plan your answer. Because this would be a seven-mark question you should not spend too much time planning. Below is an example of a key point which you might put in your plan:

There were challenges to the Kaiser but they did not lead to a challenge to his position or alter the power structure in any way. Their significance was to isolate the Kaiser further in his decision making.

Question 3

For this question you are to use the source but only as a stimulus. The question asks for an analytical answer. Therefore you need to do the following:

- Answer with a strong line of argument and make a clear judgement which comes down on one side or the other of the question.
- Show that you understand that Wilhelm's influence is considerable but should be judged in conjunction with other factors, most noticeably economic modernisation.
- Use well selected evidence to back up your argument.

Plan

Before you start writing you should plan your answer. This plan should start with the key points of argument which you will explain throughout your answer. Below are some key points which you could use as examples:

- Wilhelm's actions acted to destabilise the political system.
- Wilhelm acted to undermine the political system through his favouring the military and the lessening in influence of successive Chancellors.
- Economic modernisation and urbanisation had an important impact, most noticeable in the rise of the SPD. Political divisions arose as a result of the development of interest groups.

Style

Here is an extract from an answer to this question. Note that the candidate is attempting to be as direct as possible.

Given the evidence that Wilhelm had a central role in policy by the turn of the century it is appropriate to argue that he had a significant impact. By 1900 the Kaiser had full control over the decision making of his ministers. Most important was his manipulation of his Chancellors. Many of their actions reflected his personal prejudices and helped polarise politics. A clear example can be seen in the actions of von Bülow in 1908. In dissolving the Reichstag and creating the so-called 'Bülow-Bloc' he was simply doing the Kaiser's bidding, despite the fact that it alienated the Centre Party.

A2 SECTION: GERMANY 1848–90

INTRODUCTION

In the AS section of this book the emphasis was on a narrative of the events in Germany 1848–90. In this section the focus will be on a more detailed and in-depth analysis of the development of Germany during the period, with some evaluation of the relative importance of the various factors involved. Historical events almost invariably have complex causes, consisting of a range of different factors. It is the task of a historian to identify and explain those factors, to analyse the links between them and to evaluate their relative importance. It is also the historian's task to identify and explain the consequences of historical events. For a variety of reasons, such as the fact that evidence is often ambiguous or incomplete, or that historians approach their tasks with their own preconceptions, historians come to different conclusions when they have to interpret the evidence.

The failure of the 1848 revolutions in Germany, the unification of Germany in 1871 and the subsequent development of the Second Reich, both internally and in its relations with other powers, have been subjects on which historians have put forward different interpretations. The A2 section of this book is an attempt to explain the causes and consequences of these events and to guide the student through the interpretations put forward by the various historians who have written on the subject.

This section of the book has a chronological structure that deals with each major phase of Germany's history in turn. Within this structure, however, there are a number of underlying themes which run through the analysis.

- The development of liberalism and nationalism, the strengths and weaknesses of these movements and their contribution to the development of Germany.
- The role of Prussia in the unification of Germany and the subsequent development of the German Reich.
- The impact of social and economic change on German society and on the political system.
- The ability of an aristocratic–monarchical system of government to adapt and accommodate new forces in German society.

- The extent of opposition within the Reich and how successfully it was dealt with.

Bismarck

The role of Bismarck in the history of Germany in these years is also one of the major themes and is an issue on which historians have differed widely. Bismarck figured prominently in the story of German unification and in the development of the Second Reich between 1871 and 1890. Although most modern historians do not subscribe to the 'heroic' view of history in which great men (or women) are seen as the prime movers in historical events, it is impossible to deny that Bismarck had a major impact on the history of Germany. The importance of his role is therefore one of the major questions which has been addressed throughout this section of the book: there is a final chapter in which his legacy to the subsequent development of the German Reich is considered.

SECTION 1

Why did the German revolutions of 1848 fail?

KEY POINTS

An explanation for the failure of the German revolutions of 1848 needs to focus on four main areas.

- The sequence of events in 1848–9 and the relationship between events in Vienna, Berlin and Frankfurt.
- The nature of liberalism and the policies of the parliamentarians at Frankfurt.
- The extent of mass support for the revolutions and the attitude of the revolutionaries towards popular protest.
- The strength of conservative forces in Germany, particularly in Prussia.

HISTORICAL INTERPRETATION

Historians have been very hard on the members of the Frankfurt Parliament for their failure to lead a successful revolution and create a united country. The traditional view was that the liberal parliamentarians at Frankfurt were inexperienced intellectuals who wasted valuable time during the early months of the revolution discussing the 'Fundamental Rights of the German People' instead of taking action to bring about a united Germany. This was the view of many German historians such as **Eric Eyck** (1950) who dismissed the Frankfurt Parliament as a 'lawyers' parliament'. Writing soon after the events of 1848 the German philosopher Karl Marx argued that it was the failure of the revolutionaries to build a strong base of popular support which ensured their failure. This view has been echoed by the English historian **A.J.P. Taylor** who has written, in his provocative publication, *The Course of German History* (1961), that it was the 'divorce between the revolutionaries and the people that determined the happenings of 1848'. Most recent studies on this subject have argued that whatever mistakes were made by the parliamentarians at Frankfurt were irrelevant in determining the outcome of the struggle. The decisive events were taking place in Vienna and Berlin, not in Frankfurt.

THE SEQUENCE OF EVENTS, 1848

Revolution

The revolutions in Vienna and Berlin in March 1848 occurred against a backdrop of deepening economic crisis and the news from Paris that the French King, Louis Philippe, had been overthrown. Popular unrest and street protests, coupled with the news that a fellow monarch had been overthrown, led to a crucial failure of nerve on the part of the rulers of the Austrian Empire and the many states in Germany. In the Austrian Empire the revolution in Vienna brought about the downfall of Metternich and the promise of a constitution. In Munich the King of Bavaria was overthrown, but he was the only prince to lose his throne in Germany. Elsewhere princes and kings hastily dismissed unpopular ministers and promised reforms. In Prussia the King appointed new liberal ministers, allowed elections to be held for an Assembly and suffered the humiliation of having to salute the bodies of people killed by the army in street battles. The revolutions appeared to have transformed the political situation in Germany and ushered in a new era in which princes would share power with elected parliaments and, through agreement with the new National Assembly that began its meetings in Frankfurt in May, merge their states into a united Germany. That, at least, was the hope of the liberal parliamentarians who assembled in the *Paulskirche* in Frankfurt.

Counter-revolution

The reality was very different. Although forced to make concessions to save their thrones, the princes had not abandoned their fundamental beliefs in divine right and absolute monarchy. When the tide of revolution began to turn in the summer of 1848 the reassertion of monarchical authority was merely a matter of time. An economic revival led to a decline in popular protest. Military victories by the Austrian armies against nationalist revolts in Bohemia and in Italy inspired a growing confidence in the Empire's ruling elite. In October the Austrian general, Windischgratz, completed the rout of the revolution in Austria itself when his forces occupied Vienna. The news from Vienna stiffened the resolve of Friedrich Wilhelm IV in Prussia. In November he dismissed his liberal ministers, ordered the Prussian Parliament to leave Berlin and placed the city under martial law. By the autumn of 1848, therefore, the counter-revolution was regaining the initiative in Vienna and Berlin and by the spring of 1849 monarchical authority had been completely restored.

The real revolutions in 1848 were in Paris, Vienna and Berlin. The debates of the Frankfurt Parliament were interesting for the way in which they highlighted the problems of achieving German unity, but there was never any possibility that they could influence the outcome of events in a

Germany which was still ruled by the princes. As **Taylor** (1961) has written, 'There was no successful revolution in Germany and therefore nothing to fail. There was merely a vacuum in which the liberals postured until the vacuum was filled.' It is true that the Frankfurt Parliament spent the crucial first five months of its existence debating the 'Fundamental Rights of the German People' and only in the autumn of 1848, when the forces of counter-revolution were already gaining the initiative, did they start their discussions on the new German constitution. The constitution was not complete until the end of March 1849, by which time Friedrich Wilhelm IV in Prussia was secure enough on his throne to reject the offer of the crown of a united Germany. There were, however, good reasons for starting their work with the issue of Fundamental Rights since constitution making was dependent on an agreed statement of which rights and freedoms should be enshrined in a constitution. It was also the issue on which agreement was more likely. In any event, the question of what matters the Frankfurt Parliament should have debated first is irrelevant. The outcome of the events in Germany in 1848–9 was determined in Vienna and Berlin, not in Frankfurt.

THE NATURE AND POLICIES OF THE LIBERALS

Social background

The men who were elected to the Frankfurt Parliament were, in the words of **Carr** (1987), 'a galaxy of brilliant and talented personalities'. They included all of the leading figures in German liberalism. There were 157 lawyers or judges, 138 government officials, over 100 teachers and professors and about 40 merchants and industrialists in the Parliament. There were, however, only one peasant and four *Handwerker*. As **Grenville** (1976) has written, this was the 'most educated assembly of any parliament then in being and possibly more academic than any that has existed since'. Intellectual ability was in abundant supply; experience of government, however, was clearly lacking.

The Frankfurt Parliament was, although elected, not representative of German society at the time. The representatives were overwhelmingly middle class. Although there had been some industrial and commercial development in parts of Germany since 1815, the middle class was still but a small minority within German society as a whole. The bulk of the population were peasants. Living in the countryside and, in many areas, still trying to free themselves from feudal obligations to their landlords, the majority of peasants had very different priorities from those of the lawyers and academics who claimed, as members of the Frankfurt Parliament, to speak on behalf of the German people. The Handwerker too had grievances and demands which the parliamentarians could not begin to support or to articulate. This divorce between the Parliament and the social groups which had begun the revolution in March was the key to the outcome of the revolution.

Liberal illusions

Although the basic tenets of liberalism – belief in constitutional government with individual freedoms guaranteed by law – represented a challenge to the authority of absolute monarchies, liberalism was not essentially a revolutionary philosophy. Nineteenth-century liberals believed in the power of reasoned debate and agreed resolutions. They were legalistic and procedural in their emphasis, believing that change should be brought about through properly constituted parliamentary institutions, not by popular protest or by force of arms. This was the reason why the Frankfurt Parliament spent so long debating the issues of Fundamental Rights and the constitution. They also harboured the illusion that, with the moral authority that the Parliament had gained through being directly elected, they could persuade the princes to co-operate and agree to merge their states into a united Germany. In the early stages of the revolutions this illusion was reinforced by the willingness of the princes to make concessions. When the counter-revolution gained strength in Austria and Prussia, however, princes all over Germany began to withdraw their co-operation from the Frankfurt Parliament. The naivety of the liberals' position was then clearly exposed.

Divisions

Within the Parliament the liberals were themselves divided. The moderate majority believed in working towards agreement with the princes and in a constitution which would have a restricted franchise, thereby reducing the influence of the lower classes. There was also, however, a vociferous minority of radicals who advocated the abolition of hereditary monarchy, a democratic constitution and an aggressive foreign policy which would bring about a political crisis in Germany, thus paving the way for radical political change. The conflict between moderates and radicals came to a head in April 1848 when a leading radical from Baden, **Hecker**, attempted a revolutionary seizure of power and the establishment of a German republic. The so-called *Heckerputsch* was easily put down by the army. Another radical attempt to put pressure on the Frankfurt Parliament occurred in September after the Assembly had reluctantly agreed to accept the Prussian decision to stop the war against Denmark over Schleswig–Holstein. Radicals denounced this decision as a betrayal and a mass demonstration was called in Frankfurt to force the Parliament to change its mind. This time Austrian and Prussian troops were called in to protect the Parliament from its radical critics and from the crowds – a striking demonstration of the weakness of the Frankfurt Parliament and of its loss of moral authority.

KEY PERSON

Friedrich von Hecker A leading south-German liberal and member of the Baden Parliament. In 1847 he was the leader of a group of liberals who drew up a programme of democratic demands. These included a free press, an elected German parliament and a people's militia. In the Frankfurt Parliament Hecker was a leader of the political left. His impulsive personality led to his attempt at armed insurrection in April 1848. After the failure of the *Heckerputsch* he escaped to Switzerland and eventually settled in America.

There was also a widening gap between the liberal parliamentarians in Frankfurt and liberals in the individual states of Germany. Particularly in Prussia, liberals at state level put the need to establish constitutional government in Prussia ahead of the need to establish German unity. The debates at Frankfurt were of less importance to Prussian liberals than their own need to consolidate their position within the government of Prussia. They were also, for the most part, Prussian patriots who were loyal to the monarchy. For their part, the Frankfurt parliamentarians were aware of the dangers to German unity from a Prussia that was developing independently of the rest and were not unhappy to see Prussian liberalism crushed by Friedrich Wilhelm IV after November 1848.

Nationalism before liberalism

The majority of the members of the Frankfurt Parliament were both liberal and nationalist in their aspirations. As their attitude to the revolution in Prussia revealed, they were prepared to sacrifice political reform in the cause of German nationalism. This preference was also evident in their attitude to other nationalities. The crushing of the Czech revolt in Bohemia by the Austrian general Windischgratz was welcomed by the Frankfurt Parliament since Bohemia was regarded as an integral part of a greater Germany. They also welcomed the reassertion of Prussian authority in **Posen**. These military victories and the revival of Austrian and Prussian military power which followed them were, however, a serious threat to the liberal experiment in Germany itself. Having regained their confidence the armies then turned on the liberals in Vienna and Berlin and crushed the revolutions in Germany's two key states. In defending the German national cause in Bohemia and Posen, therefore, the liberals were encouraging the use of the same military powers which would be used later to crush them.

Fear of popular revolt

Being mainly middle class, the liberal parliamentarians at Frankfurt and the liberal leaders of revolts in the German states were solidly respectable property owners. Popular expressions of unrest such as street fighting, whilst having a value as a means of putting pressure on princes to make concessions, were a serious threat to their property. Once popular radicalism had served its purpose of forcing the princes to grant constitutions and appoint liberal ministers, those ministers and their middle-class supporters wished to prevent any further outbreaks of disorder. In Prussia, for example, the liberal ministers established a Civic Guard. Modelled on the **French National Guard**, this body was thoroughly middle class in its membership and its role was the protection of property and the suppression of revolts. The Civic Guard, however, was not equipped to perform this role adequately and the liberal ministers of Prussia were increasingly forced to rely on the Prussian army to protect them from the fury of the Berlin crowd. When the army turned on the

KEY FACT

Posen Posen had been acquired by Prussia in 1793 as part of the partition of Poland. Its population in 1848 consisted of 800,000 Poles and 500,000 Germans.

KEY TERM

French National Guard The National Guard was a part-time citizens' militia with elected officers. Composed mainly of middle-class recruits, it was originally founded in 1789 to defend the French Revolution.

HEINEMANN ADVANCED HISTORY

The disarming of the Berlin Civic Guard, November 1848.

liberal ministers in November 1848 and forced the Prussian Parliament to leave Berlin, Prussia's liberals declined the offers from the workers of Berlin to resist the counter-revolution by force. The weakness of their position was clearly exposed.

Economic policies

On economic and social questions the liberals of 1848 clung to the orthodox liberal doctrines of the time. Believing firmly in individual freedom and in the march of progress, liberals argued that the rights of private property were inviolable and that the state should not interfere in the running of business. When factory workers demanded legislation to improve working conditions or when Handwerker appealed for assistance to slow down the introduction of new machinery, their appeals were rejected by liberal parliamentarians. They were equally unsympathetic to the peasants who wanted the abolition of feudal dues or assistance in acquiring their own land from the aristocratic landowners. In short, the liberal politicians of 1848 had no social programme which could appeal to the various disaffected social groups. Indeed, they turned their backs on social unrest whenever it manifested itself and became increasingly isolated as a result.

THE EXTENT OF MASS SUPPORT

Peasants

Popular unrest, stemming from economic factors, is an essential ingredient in any revolution. The revolutions in 1848 in Germany occurred against a backdrop of long-term economic change and short-term economic crisis. The bulk of the German population lived in the countryside and earned their livings from agriculture. In rural areas, especially in the east, the pace of change was very slow and peasant farmers tended to be deeply conservative in their attitudes. Most peasants, however, were far from satisfied with their lot. In the east, there were large estates employing labourers on low wages. In the south and west, small peasant farms predominated, but increasing population put pressure on the land and forced down living standards. Feudal dues which peasants owed to their landlords were still a burden in many areas. Poor harvests in 1845–7 fuelled the discontent. Although the revolutions were mainly an urban phenomenon there were disturbances in the countryside. In the east, peasants refused to perform their feudal services and sometimes attacked castles to destroy the landowners' records. There were outbreaks of peasant unrest in the south and west also. Such revolts were leaderless and unorganised and generally ignored by the liberals in Frankfurt or Berlin.

Handwerker

The most discontented group, and the one which played the largest part in the popular unrest in the towns, were the Handwerker, artisans and craftworkers who had traditionally been the main providers of manufactured goods. The Handwerker's position was being steadily eroded by the introduction of machinery and the shift towards factory production. In the past their trades had been regulated and protected by the **guilds**, but these were in sharp decline and they had failed to persuade the princes to provide state protection as an alternative. Growing unemployment was made worse by the trade depression which began in 1847, and there had already been a number of disturbances in several towns before the outbreak of the 1848 revolutions.

The Handwerker were more organised than the peasants. In July, for example, an Artisans' Congress, with representatives from all over Germany, met in Frankfurt and demanded the control over production by the guilds. There were also links between the Handwerker and radical politicians, who invoked popular protests to strengthen their hands in the power struggle with the moderates in the Frankfurt Parliament. Such an alliance could not last, however, since the radicals were no more inclined to support the demands for a return to the guild system than were the moderates.

Factory workers

The industrial revolution in Germany was not sufficiently advanced in 1848 for factory production to be widespread. Only in Berlin and other isolated pockets of industry had large factories been established. Although working conditions in the factories were often dangerous and unpleasant, wages of factory workers were relatively high. Factory workers in Berlin

> ### KEY TERM
>
> **Guild system** The guilds were medieval organisations of craftworkers set up to regulate their trades. In particular they controlled apprenticeships as a means of restricting entry to the trades.

stood apart from the Handwerker and played very little part in the events of 1848. Karl Marx and Friedrich Engels, putative leaders of the communist movement, returned to Germany in 1848 and attempted to radicalise the revolution by fostering an alliance between working-class organisations and radical liberals. Their doctrine of class struggle failed to make much impact.

Popular protest

Popular unrest played a major role in the early stages of the revolutions. The street fighting in Berlin and the erection of barricades by the demonstrators led to the concessions made by Friedrich Wilhelm IV. Coming so soon after the news of the fall of Metternich in similar circumstances in Vienna and, with a wave of unrest sweeping through Germany in the spring of 1848, other rulers followed suit and promised constitutions. Once the crowds had done their job of forcing the princes to concede reforms the liberal politicians who assumed the leadership of the revolution had no further use for popular protest. Many rulers showed astuteness in making concessions to the peasants and, in some cases, to the Handwerker which had the effect of damping down some of the discontent. Where outbreaks of unrest continued to occur, as in the demonstrations against the Frankfurt Parliament in September after the decision to end the war in Schleswig–Holstein, order was restored by regular soldiers. Moreover, as the German economy began to revive in the summer of 1848, unemployment declined and popular discontent became less acute.

A further wave of protest swept through Germany in the spring and early summer of 1849, after the Frankfurt Parliament had been forcibly closed down. In Berlin, Breslau, Dresden and the Rhineland there were popular uprisings in defence of the federal constitution. Prussian and Saxon troops crushed these risings with little difficulty. More serious were the risings in the south-west, particularly in Baden where the Grand Duke was forced to flee. He turned to Prussia for assistance, however, and the revolt ended when Prussian forces entered the duchy and restored the Grand Duke to his throne. This marked the final collapse of the revolutions of 1848 and of the hopes of their participants.

THE STRENGTH OF CONSERVATIVE FORCES

In most successful revolutions one crucial factor is the complete internal collapse of the old regime. Rulers who have mismanaged their country's finances, lost the loyalty of their armed forces or lost the will to continue governing have been unable to withstand the shock of widespread unrest and disorder. In the German revolutions of 1848 these conditions did not apply. Most princes were not overthrown because they made tactical retreats by offering concessions. They retained control over their armies, their finances and their administrations so that real power continued to be exercised by them. Later in the year, when conditions were favourable, the princes were well placed to reassert their royal authority.

The characters of the rulers

The characters of the rulers played a part in shaping the course of events. King Ludwig I was overthrown in Bavaria because of his personal unpopularity, due largely to his open and scandalous affair with an actress, Lola Montez. The Emperor Ferdinand of Austria has been variously described by historians as 'feeble minded' and 'an imbecile'. After he was forced to abdicate in December in favour of Franz Josef the resolve of the regime to resist the forces of revolution was considerably strengthened. Friedrich Wilhelm IV of Prussia proved himself to be indecisive and inconsistent at critical moments. In March 1848, for example, his nerve failed him when street battles in Berlin led to the deaths of some rioters. He ordered his troops to withdraw from the streets, but in the confusion the army withdrew from Berlin altogether, leaving the King temporarily at the mercy of the crowds. He was humiliated by being forced to adopt the flag of the revolutionaries and to salute the dead bodies of rioters being paraded in front of him.

Supporters of monarchy

Once Friedrich Wilhelm had withdrawn to a safe distance from Berlin and taken up residence in the more aristocratic environment of Potsdam, his mood began to change. He was now surrounded by a group of conservative advisers who urged him to crush the revolution by force. The army and civil service were still loyal to the crown. The *Junker* aristocracy signalled the start of the counter-revolution when they established the League for the Protection of Landed Property in August. The news from Vienna of the crushing of the revolution by Windischgratz encouraged the King to act. In November, royal authority was restored in Prussia by the army.

Reform from above

It is important to recognise that the forces of conservatism, particularly in Prussia, were not merely reactionaries who attempted to put the clock back. Friedrich Wilhelm wanted a reformed and strengthened system of government in which the King's right to rule would be recognised but the basic freedoms of his subjects would be enshrined in law. Hence, one of the positive outcomes of 1848–9 was that Prussia emerged with a new constitution, albeit one which had been granted by royal favour. Conservatives also proved more sympathetic to the demands of the Handwerker. In February 1849 Prussia introduced legislation restoring the guild system and other states followed suit. The peasants, too, benefited from the abolition of feudal dues in Prussia in April 1849 and in other states soon after. It was no surprise, therefore, when the Prussian army, largely made up of peasant recruits, suppressed the revolts in the summer of 1849.

CONCLUSION

There was very little prospect of a successful revolution in Germany in 1848. Popular unrest did result in outbreaks of street fighting, but these were sporadic and confined to the main cities in a territory where most of the people lived in the countryside. Peasants' loyalties remained with the princes, especially after some princes removed feudal dues. The liberals who assumed the leadership of the revolt based their strategies on false assumptions, most notably the illusion that parliamentary government and national unity could be achieved through agreement with the princes. When the princes made clear their refusal to abide by the resolutions of the Frankfurt Parliament, the parliamentarians themselves had no alternative strategy in mind. They shrank from taking the only step which might have had some chance of success – leading a popular revolt against the princes – because they valued order and property as much as the landowning aristocracy. Monarchical power in the German states, despite suffering a crisis of confidence in the first weeks of the revolutions, remained firmly entrenched. Crucially, the King of Prussia and the Emperor of Austria retained control of their armies and were able to launch counter-revolutions to regain the political initiative within their own states. Once the revolutions in Vienna and Berlin had been crushed it was only a matter of time before the Frankfurt Parliament was made to face the realities of power in Germany at that time.

SECTION 2

Why was German unification achieved through Prussian victory?

KEY POINTS

An explanation of the reasons for, and the nature of, German unification in 1871 needs to focus on five main questions.

- What was the extent of popular support for unification and what role did this play in the events of 1862–71?
- How did economic factors contribute to the success of Prussia?
- What role did military factors play in the success of Prussia?
- What were the weaknesses of the other states?
- How important was Bismarck in the story of German unification?

HISTORICAL INTERPRETATION

Historians writing about the unification of Germany in the 1860s have tended to focus on the role of Bismarck and on the victories of the Prussian army. This is understandable since the declaration of the German Reich in 1871 followed the victories of the Prussian army over Austria in 1866 and France in 1871, events in which it seemed that Bismarck was setting the diplomatic agenda. Traditional historiography on this subject emphasised the role of Bismarck as the architect of unification, but more recent work has also supported this view: **Gall** (1986) and **Craig** (1981) place Bismarck at the centre of the story. Other historians have approached the story of German unification from different perspectives, seeing it as the culmination of a long process in which the rise of national consciousness, the growth of Prussia's economic power and the role of the Prussian army are all given greater prominence. Bohme (in a 1966 German work) and **Henderson** (1975) have emphasised the importance of economic factors whilst, in a recent article in *Modern History Review*, **Michael John** (1991) has argued for greater emphasis to be given to the role of popular support for unification.

THE EXTENT OF POPULAR SUPPORT FOR UNIFICATION

Nationalverein

German national feeling revived after the war scare of 1859, a development which was reflected in the establishment of the *Nationalverein*. This new organisation, which had links with the national congresses of economists, chambers of commerce and lawyers, led the way in the 1860s in calling for German unification under the leadership of Prussia. The Nationalverein also had links with liberal and progressive parties which were gaining support in various German states, including Prussia, in the early 1860s. Thus, the Nationalverein can legitimately be seen as an organised expression of German national consciousness at a time when the issue of German unification was once again coming to the fore in German politics. The weakness of the Nationalverein, however, was that its support was limited; at its height it had only 25,000 members and most of those were from the professions and the propertied middle class. Although it would be a mistake to dismiss the Nationalverein as irrelevant, since it was a vehicle for the articulate and educated middle class to express their clear preference for a united Germany on a *Kleindeutsch* basis, its influence over the course of events was undeniably limited.

Popular patriotism

In his article **Michael John** (1991) has argued that there was another dimension to popular support for unification. Although German politics at this time were overwhelmingly local and regional in scope, there were opportunities for ordinary Germans to express national pride. A series of anniversaries in the early 1860s provided outlets for such feelings; the centenaries of the births of the poet Schiller (1859) and the philosopher Fichte (1862) were celebrated through festivals at which national feelings were strongly expressed. Similarly, the fiftieth anniversaries of the victories over Napoleon at Leipzig (1813) and Waterloo (1815) were opportunities for celebrations of national pride. During the 1850s and 1860s also there was an increase in membership of singing, shooting and gymnastics clubs. Although their activities were primarily recreational and these clubs disavowed any involvement in politics, they were suspected at the time of being front organisations for liberal and nationalist political groups. Whilst these suspicions were probably unfounded the clubs were 'political' in the broadest sense. In other words, their members shared a strong sense of patriotism and a desire for greater German unity. In disavowing politics they were refusing to take sides in the debate between *Kleindeutsch* and *Grossdeutsch* nationalism.

Schleswig–Holstein crisis

The Schleswig–Holstein crisis brought about the biggest mobilisation of popular nationalism seen in Germany since 1848. Public meetings held to support the claims of the Duke of Augustenberg sometimes attracted as many as 10,000 people. Schleswig–Holstein Associations sprang up all over Germany and a Committee of Thirty-Six was established to lead the campaign. Since 1862 the Nationalverein had had a rival organisation in the shape of the *Reformverein* which had been created to press the case for a Grossdeutsch solution to national unity. On the Schleswig–Holstein issue both organisations sank their differences and co-operated to press the German nationalist cause. The limitations of the nationalist movement were clearly exposed, however, when both Austria and Prussia refused to recognise the claims of the Duke of Augustenberg and pursued their own interests. The failure of the nationalists to influence the outcome of the Schleswig–Holstein crisis caused both the Nationalverein and the Reformverein to go into decline, with the latter collapsing altogether as the case for a Grossdeutsch solution was fatally undermined by the success of Prussia in the coming years.

There is some evidence, therefore, that popular nationalism in Germany was more widespread than historians have traditionally acknowledged. **John** (1991) has argued that 'the growing dominance of nationalist rhetoric as the basic currency of German political debate' formed the essential backdrop to Bismarck's political manoeuvres in the years 1862–71. Undoubtedly, there were many nationalists who welcomed the success of Prussia in creating the German Reich in 1871 whilst there is equally clear evidence of the unpopularity of Bismarck's policies among other nationalists. What is quite clear, however, particularly in the light of the Schleswig–Holstein crisis, is how little influence popular nationalism had over the outcome of events.

WHAT PART DID ECONOMIC FACTORS PLAY IN THE PROCESS OF UNIFICATION?

The Zollverein

With hindsight it is possible to see the *Zollverein* as inspired by a desire for greater national unity and as an institution that inexorably tied other German states to Prussia economically long before political unity was achieved. The fact that the Zollverein was established under Prussian leadership and that Austria was excluded can be seen as setting the scene for an eventual Prussian takeover of Germany. Whilst the Zollverein was undoubtedly important in establishing Prussian economic leadership in Germany, its role in bringing about the unification of Germany should not be exaggerated.

Prussian origins. The first moves towards the establishment of the Zollverein were made by Prussia after the end of the Napoleonic wars. In 1815 Prussia had gained territory in the Rhineland which was separated from the rest of the state by Hanover, Hesse-Cassel, Hesse-Darmstadt and Nassau. In order to integrate the western provinces with the rest of Prussia and to stimulate economic development throughout the country, the Prussian government needed to develop communications links through the territories of these other states and to break down customs barriers which impeded trade. In 1818 Prussia introduced a liberal tariff regime that abolished internal customs barriers and reduced import and export duties within its own territory. This Zollverein was extended in 1819 to include the enclaves of other states' territories within Prussia's borders and, in 1828, to include Hesse-Darmstadt. In the early stages of the formation of the Zollverein, therefore, it was Prussia's own internal needs which provided the driving force, not any desire to seize the economic leadership in Germany.

Expansion of the Zollverein. A much enlarged Zollverein was formed in 1834 when eighteen other states, including Bavaria, Wurttemberg, Thuringia and Saxony, joined. Prussian leadership was assured by the fact that it was the Prussian tariff which was adopted by the other member states and that Prussia represented the other states in trade negotiations with foreign powers. The arrangement was not permanent. Initially the Zollverein was to last for eight years; thereafter, it was renewed every twelve years. Member states still retained their sovereignty over their economic affairs, but in practice Prussia usually won any arguments by applying pressure on the smaller states.

Along with the German Confederation, the Zollverein was the only national institution in Germany in the years before unification. Unlike the Confederation there was no compulsion on German states to join and, in a gesture of resistance to Prussian economic dominance, Hanover formed a rival customs union with a number of smaller states. The success of the Zollverein in stimulating trade and increasing the customs revenue available to the member states persuaded the Hanoverians to merge their rival union into the Zollverein in 1852. Thus, by the 1850s the only major German state outside the Zollverein was Austria. In 1852 the Austrian government proposed an all-German customs union and won support for its proposal from many German states. Initially, Prussia refused to participate in negotiations on the Austrian proposal, but eventually a compromise was reached whereby a commercial treaty was concluded between Austria and the Zollverein. Austrian membership had been blocked by the Prussians whose economic leadership of Germany was thereby underlined.

Rivalry with Austria. Prussia's decision to establish the Zollverein without Austria and then to resist Austrian attempts to submerge it within a wider, Austrian-dominated customs union can be seen as consistent with a long-term Prussian ambition to challenge Austria's leadership in

Germany. As has been shown, however, the establishment of the Zollverein had more to do with Prussia's own internal needs than with its wish to dominate neighbouring states. The decision to exclude Austria, particularly during the 1850s and 1860s, was only partially connected with the wider political rivalry between the two states. There were also sound economic reasons for doing so. As Prussia began to industrialise in the 1850s its economy grew further apart from that of Austria, which remained a predominantly agrarian society. Prussia and the Zollverein were moving towards free trade whilst Austria remained committed to trade protection. With Austria and Prussia in the same customs union conflicts of interest would have been inevitable and the smooth running of the union could not be guaranteed.

Success of the Zollverein. The success of the Zollverein made the German states more economically interdependent. It also showed that even more rapid economic growth could be achieved if other aspects of economic life such as postal systems, railways, currency and weights and measures were brought under unified control. It is undoubtedly the case, therefore, that the experience of the Zollverein gave many Germans, particularly industrialists and merchants, a practical demonstration of the advantages of unification. This did not necessarily mean that the business interests in states such as Bavaria and Hanover were in favour of political unification on Prussia's terms. The governments of these states were even less inclined to see membership of the Zollverein as a first step towards a German Reich dominated by Prussia. The small and medium-sized German states could best preserve their independence by using Austria and Prussia as counterweights within the overall balance of power. Austria's political leadership of the Confederation was counterbalanced by Prussia's economic leadership of the Zollverein. Membership of the Zollverein did not imply support for Prussia's political ambitions, as was demonstrated in 1866 when most of the smaller states in the Zollverein, including Hanover, supported Austria in the war against Prussia.

Railways

The role of the railways in breaking down barriers to trade and engendering a greater sense of national unity has been described in Chapter 1. The railways stimulated economic growth and the development of economic interdependence among the separate states of Germany. Berlin became one of the major railway centres with lines radiating out to all parts of Germany, strengthening the position of the city as a major centre of commerce and industry long before it became the imperial capital.

Strategic value. The early railway lines in Germany were built piecemeal, without any overall plan by any state or by the Zollverein. The strategic value of railways in moving armies to the front with speed and efficiency was quickly understood by the Prussian army's General Staff. Their view was confirmed by the war of 1859 between France and Austria. One of the factors behind the French victory was the speed with which they were able to assemble their forces by using railways. During the early 1860s there was a boom in the building of strategic railway lines in Prussia, a process in which the army General Staff played a leading role. During the war of 1866 the Prussian army had five railway lines at its disposal to move its troops into position over a front of 350 miles. The Austrians had only two railway lines on their side of the front, with the result that the Austrian commanders were hampered by having far less mobility than their Prussian counterparts. The mobility of Prussian forces was one of the factors in their victory.

Industrial strength

German industrial expansion after 1815 occurred largely in Prussian territory. The main industrial areas of the Ruhr, Silesia and the Saarland were all in Prussia, which therefore had a preponderance of coal mines, iron and steel-making capacity and engineering works over other German states. Prussia's growing steel-making and engineering capabilities made possible the rapid improvements in weapons technology. The firm of Krupps of Essen was one of the key factors behind Prussia's military success in the 1860s and 1870s.

The growing economic strength of Prussia, together with its leadership of the Zollverein, shifted the balance of economic power within Germany in Prussia's favour. The wealth generated by industrial expansion made it possible for the Prussian state to maintain, supply and equip a large army with which to fight the three wars which led to the unification of Germany in 1871. It should be noted, however, that both Austria and France had experienced economic growth and both of these powers were able to field large armies in 1866 and 1870 respectively. Economic strength alone cannot explain the victories of Prussia's armies in those wars.

WHY WAS THE PRUSSIAN ARMY SO SUCCESSFUL IN THE WARS OF GERMAN UNIFICATION?

The wars of 1864, 1866 and 1870–1 all resulted in decisive victories for the Prussian armies in the field. Only in the war against Denmark was there an overwhelming superiority in numbers for the Prussian forces, and on that occasion the small Danish army was facing the combined military might of Prussia and the Austrian Empire. In 1866, 221,000 Prussian soldiers faced 215,000 Austrians and Saxons, a small numerical advantage but not large enough to affect the outcome of the war. In 1870 the French had large reserves of manpower at their disposal but their inability to mobilise their reserves and move them into position with the same speed as the Prussians was a key factor. Whereas Prussia had 460,000 men under arms and in position within the first few weeks of the war, the French could only muster 240,000 out of a potential 400,000 within the same period.

Organisation and planning

The Prussian Chief of Staff, von Moltke, made a major contribution to Prussia's military victories through the preparation and planning which he had instigated since the early 1860s. In the army reforms which precipitated the political crisis of 1862 von Moltke had not only increased the size of the Prussian army. Other reforms improved the tactical mobility of the army on the battlefield by giving greater responsibility to junior officers and non-commissioned officers (NCOs). He also greatly improved the provision of supplies for an army in the field by establishing separate supply units, specialist railway units and field bakeries. The command structure was also overhauled to give field commanders more initiative within the overall strategic plan devised by the General Staff. The Prussian army was able to supply its field commanders with detailed and accurate maps of the areas in which they were fighting, both in 1866 and in 1870. The French officers, on the other hand, were only supplied with maps of German territory despite the fact that they were actually fighting in France. The French had no detailed mobilisation plan and their supplies were inadequate to maintain an army in the field.

Helmut von Moltke, Prussian Chief of Staff.

Technology

The technological gap between the Prussian army and its adversaries also played a part in the victories. Of particular importance in this context was the quality of the weaponry deployed by the respective armies. Prussia had introduced the breech-loading Dreyse gun in 1843 when other armies were still equipped with muskets. In the war of 1866 Prussian soldiers had three times the rate of fire with their weapons compared with the Austrians: this superiority of firepower was a major factor in the stunning victory of the Prussian army at Koniggratz, near Sadowa. The Prussians also used artillery with rifled barrels for the first time in 1866. These weapons had a far longer range and greater accuracy than the smooth-bored cannons with which the Austrians were equipped. The Prussians were not properly trained in their use, however, and were unable to exploit their advantage to the full. During the next three years the Prussian army undertook a major training programme to improve use of the new technology.

In the war of 1870 it was the French who had superior firepower with their *chassepot* infantry rifle. They were unable to take full advantage of the weapon's capabilities because of the superior Prussian tactics on the battlefield.

Political and diplomatic context

Once wars begin the quality of preparation and planning, weaponry and tactics become decisive factors in the outcome of battles. The wars of 1864, 1866 and 1870–1 were all won by Prussian armies which had clear military advantages over their opponents, but they were also won because of the favourable diplomatic situation in which they were fought. In the war against Denmark no foreign power intervened, despite the Treaty of London of 1852 in which Great Britain accepted responsibility for guaranteeing the status of Schleswig–Holstein. Bismarck was careful throughout the crisis not to place Prussia in clear breach of the Treaty of London and, once the war had begun, he restrained the army from invading Denmark itself. Such an extension of the war might well have widened the conflict.

In the war of 1866, as a result of Bismarck's diplomatic manoeuvrings, Austria had to fight a war on two fronts and without any major powers as allies. Italian intervention had been achieved through the alliance concluded only weeks before and French and Russian neutrality had been secured by Bismarck with careful diplomacy. Bismarck was keenly aware, however, that French neutrality could not be guaranteed if Prussia's victory was so overwhelming as to threaten the very existence of the Austrian Empire. He therefore had to restrain von Moltke and the King from pressing on to Vienna after the victory at Koniggratz. Bismarck feared that the longer the war went on the more likely foreign

The Austrian and Prussian armies meet on the battlefield of Koniggratz.

intervention became and he had to assert the primacy of political decision making over the purely military considerations which were uppermost in von Moltke's mind once the war had begun.

A similar battle between von Moltke and Bismarck was fought during the Franco-Prussian war of 1870–1. Once again Bismarck had not acted until he was sure that the French would be isolated in this war, but he was also aware that the longer the war continued the more risk there was of outside intervention. Bismarck complained to the King that von Moltke did not keep him informed about the military situation in France, and without such information Bismarck could not keep overall control of the political direction of the war. Eventually, after a long struggle, Bismarck won the King's backing and von Moltke was ordered to keep Bismarck fully informed. It was Bismarck who pressed von Moltke to bombard Paris with his artillery in January 1871 in order to bring the war to a speedy conclusion and it was Bismarck who decided to stop the bombardment at the end of January when French political representatives indicated their willingness to begin peace negotiations. Once again Bismarck had averted the risk of outside intervention by limiting the scale and extent of the conflict.

WHAT WERE THE WEAKNESSES OF THE OTHER GERMAN STATES?

Prussia's military victories over Austria and other German states in 1866 were assisted by the comparative weaknesses of those states. States such as Hanover and Saxony were much smaller in size than Prussia and had more limited resources. Prussia's victories over these states, therefore, were not a surprise.

Weaknesses of the Austrian Empire

Less expected was the speed and decisiveness of the victory over Austria since the Austrian Empire had a larger population than Prussia and considerable economic potential. The Austrian Empire, however, suffered from serious internal problems that gravely weakened the armies which took the field against Prussian forces in 1866.

Economic problems. The first of these problems was economic. Following the defeat of the revolutions of 1848–9, monarchical authority was restored in the Austrian Empire and, during the 1850s, a more centralised system of government was introduced. Under the new Emperor Franz Josef and his ministers, Schwarzenberg and Bach, order was restored and decision making concentrated in the hands of the imperial government. Reform from above brought about the development of railways and roads, the beginnings of a free-trade area within the Empire, the expansion of industry and foreign trade and the emancipation of the peasants from feudal dues. All of these reforms stimulated economic activity and created the conditions for increasing prosperity during the 1850s. However, Austria's failure to gain admittance to the Zollverein, together with the problem of poor communications with the more economically developed regions of northern and western Europe, meant that Austria's external trade and its overall economic development were held back. By the 1860s it was clear that the economic development of the Empire was failing to fulfil its earlier promise.

Political difficulties. There were also serious political difficulties in a multinational empire that was struggling to contain the growth of nationalist feelings among its various nationalities. Despite the defeat of nationalist revolts in Italy, Bohemia and Hungary in 1848–9, the Austrian Empire continued to experience difficulties with its subject nations. Defeat in Italy and the loss of Lombardy in 1859 sparked a political crisis in the Empire that was not resolved until the *Ausgleich* of 1867. The first steps towards fundamental change were taken in 1861 when the Emperor, Franz Josef, issued the February Patent which authorised a number of reforms. Local representative institutions were set up and from these delegates were to be elected to a *Reichsrat* (imperial council). This was the first parliamentary institution for the Austrian Empire but its powers were limited. The Hungarians, in particular, were not prepared to recognise the authority of the Reichsrat and refused to send delegates to it. Moreover, Hungarian resentment at the centralisation of power in the Empire led to a widespread refusal to pay taxes, and 150,000 troops had to be kept in Hungary in order to maintain Austrian control. The wider implications for the Empire of this continuing internal unrest had already been seen in the war of 1859 when Hungarian and Italian troops in the imperial army deserted in large numbers. Continuing doubt over the loyalty of Hungarian troops was a serious handicap for the Austrian Empire when it faced a war with Prussia in 1866.

Military weakness. The refusal of Hungarians to pay taxes added to an already serious shortfall in the revenue of the imperial government. Tax revenues had, for some time, been insufficient to pay the costs of administration and of the army. The reforms of the 1850s had failed to solve this problem and when, after 1859, the Empire needed to expand and re-equip its army to meet the serious internal and external challenges it was now facing, financial constraints prevented this from happening. In the war of 1866, therefore, the Austrian army was under-strength and equipped with outdated muzzle-loading rifles. The army was also poorly led. Officers in the Austrian army were selected not on the basis of their ability but on their social standing. Many of the aristocratic officers chosen by Franz Josef to lead the army were not equal to the task.

Ausgleich
Following defeat in 1866 the stability and survival of the Austrian Empire were under threat. In an historic compromise, known as the *Ausgleich*, the Emperor agreed to share power within the Empire between the Austrians and the Hungarians. Henceforth the Empire was known as the Austro-Hungarian Empire and Franz Josef ruled as Emperor of Austria and King of Hungary.

The Austrian Empire faced its most severe test in the war against Prussia in 1866 in a divided and weakened state. Whereas in Prussia a constitutional crisis had been used by Bismarck to the advantage of the state by facing down the liberals and appealing to their nationalism, in Austria nationalism was at the heart of the crisis. Conflict with the Italians and the Hungarians sapped the confidence and the strength of the Empire at a critical moment in its history.

HOW IMPORTANT WAS BISMARCK IN THE PROCESS OF GERMAN UNIFICATION?

Bismarck was regarded by many of his contemporaries, and by subsequent generations of Germans, as the founder of the Second Reich. This was an impression which he himself was keen to perpetuate in his autobiography, published after his resignation in 1890, in which he emphasised his own role in the events of the 1860s. Many historians and biographers have placed him at the centre of the events, stressing the skill and cunning of his handling of the complex and contradictory forces both in Prussia itself and in the wider European context. It would be impossible to tell the story of German unification without giving Bismarck's role due prominence, but it is also important to acknowledge that Bismarck was working within a political, diplomatic, social and economic context which he did not create and over which he did not have complete mastery. Between 1862 and 1871 the map of Germany was altered radically and Bismarck played a key role in the events which led to the foundation of the new Reich, but his success was due to a combination of factors, not simply his own skill and genius as a politician.

Bismarck's Realpolitik

According to one of his biographers, **Otto Pflanze** (1963), Bismarck was 'driven by a vital compulsion to seize the helm and steer'. His deep religious convictions led him to the belief that, by himself, the individual can create nothing but that it was his moral duty to try to accomplish what he could. Bismarck was a Junker landowner who first made his mark in Prussian politics as a reactionary defender of the status quo when he was elected to the United Diet in 1847. During the events of 1848–9 his reputation as a die-hard defender of the old order was enhanced by his public statements in favour of the monarchy and the Confederation and his attacks on the liberal nationalists at Frankfurt. But he also learned from the experiences of 1848 that ideals have to be made practical through compromises with reality. He was beginning to develop and refine the political philosophy which has come to be closely identified with the name of Bismarck, *Realpolitik*. The essence of this was summed up in the statement he made in 1850: 'The only sound foundation of a great state . . . is state egoism and not romanticism . . . it is unworthy of a great state to fight for something in which it has no interest'.

As a Prussian and a loyal servant of the Prussian King, he placed the interests of the Prussian state at the top of his list of priorities. Whatever promoted the interests of Prussia was justified in Bismarck's eyes. His overriding aim throughout the 1850s and 1860s was to establish Prussian dominance in northern Germany – something which would inevitably involve a struggle with Austria. He was not, however, hell-bent on provoking a war with Austria. War was always one possible solution to the problem, but Bismarck regarded it as a last resort, to be used only when all other options had been exhausted. Bismarck was not a German nationalist but he recognised in the growth of nationalism, particularly after the setting up of the Nationalverein in 1859, a force which could be enlisted on the side of Prussia in the struggles which lay ahead.

Otto von Bismarck.

Early career

During the 1850s Bismarck served the Prussian state as its representative at the Confederation Diet and later as Ambassador to Russia. After the Prussian attempt to establish the Erfurt Union and the humiliation of Olmutz, relations between Prussia and Austria were severely strained. The Austrians abandoned the policy which they had pursued before 1848 of close co-operation with Prussia in the Confederation and opted to reassert their predominance in Germany. Bismarck's response was to adopt an aggressive policy of obstructionism towards the Austrians in an attempt to force them to treat Prussia as an equal. He wrote a series of memoranda to the King advising him to take every opportunity to seize the leadership in Germany, but his advice was not heeded. He was treated as a brilliant misfit whose ideas were either eccentric or dangerous, and when he was appointed Minister-President of Prussia in 1862 it was not his policies which were his main qualification for the job so much as his reputation as a strong man who was capable of defying the opposition.

First steps in power

When he took over control of Prussian foreign policy in 1862 there was no dramatic change of direction. His policies of challenging Austria and trying to establish friendly relations with France and Russia had all been pursued by his predecessor. His first year in office was not an outstanding success. His clumsy intervention in the Polish revolt in an attempt to cultivate Russia's friendship only served to antagonise the Russian government. Relations with Austria were already strained when Bismarck took office and he made the rift even deeper by thwarting the Austrian plan to reform the German Confederation. This at least was consistent with Bismarck's aim to challenge Austrian leadership in Germany. Relations with Austria continued to deteriorate from this point.

Schleswig–Holstein

It was the issue of Schleswig–Holstein which brought relations between Prussia and Austria to a crisis point and led to war in 1864. Bismarck was not planning for war in 1864 when the crisis first began, nor could he have predicted how the situation would develop. It was the Danes who precipitated the crisis by attempting to incorporate Schleswig into Denmark. Germany was swept by a wave of popular indignation and national feeling which crystallised into a demand for the Confederation to defend German interests in the duchies. Bismarck was unmoved by the demonstrations. Prussian self-interest, not popular sentiment, was the basis of his policy. He kept the possibility of annexing Schleswig–Holstein in mind from the beginning and worked towards this end, but other solutions were not ruled out. The worst possible outcome for Prussia, he believed, would be the establishment of an independent Schleswig–Holstein which would be under Austrian influence. Allowing the duchies to remain under Danish rule would be preferable to having greater Austrian influence in northern Germany.

The 'strategy of alternatives'

Characteristically, Bismarck adopted a cautious approach. He believed that an indispensable quality in a statesman was patience. 'We can set our watches', he once wrote, 'but the time passes no more quickly because of that, and the ability to wait while conditions develop is a requisite of practical policy.' His approach to power politics has been described as the 'strategy of alternatives'(**Pflanze**, 1963). He kept open many possible solutions to political problems, each of which could be explored until the moment of final choice. In that way he could weigh up the possible consequences of each course of action and evaluate the intentions and the strengths and weaknesses of his opponents. He also believed that there were critical moments in foreign policy which 'never come again' and at those moments it was the statesman's duty to act decisively and make the most of the opportunities that had been presented to him.

His cautious approach in the early stages of the Schleswig–Holstein crisis kept Prussian policy within the bounds of the 1852 Treaty of London so that other powers would not have a pretext for intervention. The alliance with Austria gave the impression that Prussian ambitions had been contained whereas in reality Austrian support had been enlisted to further Prussia's interests. These aspects of Bismarck's policy show the flexibility and dexterity which were characteristic of his strategy of alternatives, an approach which he employed with great skill to manoeuvre the situation to Prussia's advantage. Again we must be careful not to exaggerate the element of conscious planning in Bismarck's handling of the situation, nor to overestimate the impact which Bismarck's policies alone could have on a complex situation. Danish intransigence removed the possibility of finding a compromise that was unfavourable to Prussia;

Austria's defensive approach allowed Bismarck to take the initiative. He was also fortunate in facing an exceptionally favourable international situation. No great power was prepared to fight for Denmark and relations between the powers were more fluid than they had been for decades.

Relations with Austria

Relations between Prussia and Austria had reached a critical point after the Danish war and the compromise over Schleswig–Holstein. Bismarck never lost sight of his basic aim of forcing Austria to concede the leadership over northern Germany to Prussia, but a war between the two powers was not the only possible outcome of this struggle. In Bismarck's mind was the possibility that Austria might be persuaded to concede if sufficient pressure were applied. After the war with France in 1859 Austria was virtually bankrupt; there was still the possibility of another war over **Venetia** and the Austrian Empire was isolated within Europe. Thus, whilst increasing the pressure on Austria through diplomatic links with France and an alliance with Italy, Bismarck pursued a careful, measured approach towards Austria itself. In the event it was Austria which gave Prussia a pretext for war by breaking the terms of the Gastein Convention when the Austrian government asked the German Confederation to decide the future of the duchies. The war of 1866 may appear with hindsight to have been the inevitable and planned result of Bismarck's policies over the previous two years, but not all of the factors which led to the outbreak of hostilities were within Bismarck's control.

War with France

Diplomatic tensions. War with France was the final step on the road to German unification. Bismarck believed that the unification of the southern states with the North German Confederation was inevitable, but he had no firm plans as to when and how this could be accomplished. With strong popular resistance to unification in the south final unification did not appear, in the late 1860s, to be a practical possibility in the short term. Once again Bismarck was prepared to wait on events and concentrate on consolidating the unity of the new North German Confederation. The French government, feeling strongly that France had suffered as a result of the Prussian victory in 1866 and its consequences for the balance of power, was determined to resist any further expansion of Prussia. After the Luxembourg crisis of 1867 relations between Prussia and France deteriorated and there was growing tension between them. War was a possible outcome of this tension, but Bismarck was not looking for war, nor did he believe that Louis Napoleon desired it. Disagreements with France and the potential for future conflict between the two powers, however, were useful to Bismarck because he could exploit the tension to arouse national feeling in Germany and to persuade the southern states to accept closer military co-operation with Prussia.

KEY FACT

Venetia Until 1859 Lombardy and Venetia in northern Italy were part of the Austrian Empire. The war of 1859 in which France and Piedmont sought to force Austria to give up its two Italian provinces was only partially successful. The new Kingdom of Italy, therefore, still wished to gain control of Venetia.

Hohenzollern candidature. When Bismarck supported the Hohenzollern candidature for the Spanish throne he was well aware that this would provoke a hostile reaction from France. He was almost certainly ready to risk war but this was not the only possible outcome of the crisis. A diplomatic humiliation for France would serve his purposes just as well. The development of the crisis to the point where war became inevitable was due as much to the clumsy and incautious way in which the French government handled the issue as it was to Bismarck's actions.

- Napoleon III, facing a serious decline in his personal popularity and an increasingly unstable regime, needed a foreign-policy triumph to strengthen his own position. The French, therefore, were not content to accept the mere withdrawal of the candidature, but pressed for guarantees that it would never be renewed.
- Wilhelm I was prepared to oblige the French over their first demand – he had not been fully convinced of the wisdom of the candidature from the beginning – but he regarded their demand for guarantees as a slur on his honour.
- Bismarck had suffered a serious diplomatic defeat when the candidature was withdrawn, but the French blunder over the guarantees issue and Bismarck's opportunistic behaviour in editing the Ems telegram enabled him to turn a defeat into a triumph.
- Even then the final decision to declare war was made by the French government. Pressure from newspapers and outraged members of the Chamber of Deputies pushed the government into declaring war on Prussia.

The victory of Prussia, its alliance with the southern states and the unleashing of a wave of popular nationalism across Germany led to the creation of the German Reich in 1871. This was an outcome with which Bismarck would have been highly satisfied because it had been achieved by the expansion of Prussia, but it was not something which he could have planned or predicted when he became Minister-President of Prussia in 1862.

CONCLUSION

It is impossible to explain the process of German unification without emphasising the role played by Bismarck. In the complex political and diplomatic situation of the 1860s, both inside Prussia and in its dealings with the German states and other European powers, Bismarck displayed great skill and dexterity. He had a clear view of his aims and the absolute conviction that his methods could be justified by the extent to which they served the interests of the Prussian state. We should not, however, see Bismarck as infallible. He made mistakes in his first year in office and his diplomacy was not always successful. The Hohenzollern candidature nearly ended in humiliation for Bismarck, but he was rescued by the blunders of the French and his own opportunism.

We must also place Bismarck's achievements in their proper context in order to fully appreciate the extent of his importance.

- Firstly, we must recognise that Bismarck's policies were not unique to him or original. In his advice to his monarch he frequently referred to the traditional rivalry with Austria and Prussia's long tradition of expansion in northern Germany, trends which dated back to the time of Friedrich the Great in the 18th century.
- Secondly, Prussia's ability to challenge Austria depended on its military strength and on its economic resources, both of which had been built up by Prussian governments over generations before Bismarck came upon the scene. It was the awareness of Prussia's strength which gave Bismarck the confidence to assert Prussia's claims in his dealings with Austria, and later France.
- Thirdly, Bismarck was fortunate in facing an unusually favourable European diplomatic situation in the 1860s when Prussia was challenging the existing balance of power. A hostile coalition of powers could at any time have thwarted Prussia's ambitions; the fact that this did not occur was only partially due to Bismarck's skill as a diplomat.
  - The Crimean war had disrupted the long-standing conservative axis of Austria and Russia, the factor which had decisively ended the threat to the Austrian Empire in 1848–9 and led to the restoration of Austrian influence in Germany.
  - Feeling that they had been betrayed by Austria during the Crimean war, the Russians were in no mood to intervene to support the Austrian Empire in Germany in 1866.
  - Across Europe there was an almost universal distrust of Napoleon III. Although this did not preclude France finding allies it was a factor which Bismarck was able to exploit.
  - Great Britain, in the mid-1860s, was reluctant to become involved in the conflicts in continental Europe.

Prussia, in Bismarck's estimation, occupied a position at the fulcrum of the European balance of power and, with relations between the powers in such a fluid state, Prussia had more room for manoeuvre. Bismarck displayed skill in playing off one power against the others but he was fortunate in that he was operating within a context in which the whole balance of power was being challenged from several directions simultaneously.

SECTION 3

How united was the German Reich?

KEY POINTS

After the creation of the Second Reich in 1871 conflicts of economic interest, religious controversy, class conflict and political factionalism all had the potential to divide the loyalties of the German people and undermine the unity of the Reich. To understand whether or not Germany's rulers established a stable political system which could reconcile these differences we must consider four main questions.

- How well did the constitution promote greater unity?
- How successful was Bismarck in promoting unity?
- How did social and economic change affect the cohesion of the German Reich?
- How did Germany's rulers cope with the consequences of social and economic change?

THE PROBLEM

When the German Reich (Empire) was created in 1871 it was achieved by the force of Prussian arms over the opposition of entrenched forces in other German states. Despite the charade acted out at Versailles when Wilhelm I was 'invited' by the other German princes to adopt the title of German Kaiser (Emperor), the unification of Germany was imposed by Prussia. As we have seen, there were strong forces in Germany that were pressing for greater political unity, particularly the industrial and commercial middle class, and the war against France had unleashed a wave of patriotic German feeling that revealed an underlying current of support for a united Germany. Opposition to unification, however, was also very strong, particularly among the rulers of the German states which would lose their identity within the new Reich. Particularism was present in all parts of Germany but was strongest in the southern states. If the new Reich were to fulfil its role of providing a focus of loyalty for all Germans these differences would have to be accommodated within its constitutional structure.

Germany was a large and diverse country. There were significant regional differences between north and south and between east and west. Recent economic development had widened the difference between the more

The Proclamation of the German Reich in the Hall of Mirrors at Versailles, 1871.

industrialised western part of Germany and the more agrarian east. This gap would continue to widen in the first twenty years of the Reich's history as industrialisation gathered speed. Religious diversity also divided the nation and tended to reinforce the gap between the north and the south and the east and the west. The inclusion of small but significant national minorities within the Reich – Poles, Danes and the inhabitants of Alsace–Lorraine – added to the cultural diversity of Germany but had the potential for weakening the unity of the state. German society also exhibited wide class differences and the gap between classes was increasing because of rapid social and economic change.

HOW WELL DID THE CONSTITUTION PROMOTE GREATER UNITY?

The constitution of the Reich was a compromise between the entrenched power of the princes and the pressure for greater political freedom and national unity which was represented by the National Liberal party. Sovereignty within the Reich continued to reside with the 22 princes who, in theory at least, created the Reich by an act of voluntary association and presented it as a gift to the German people. The power of the princes to protect their particularist interests was enshrined in the Bundesrat (federal council). Local state governments retained not inconsiderable powers over education, justice, agriculture, relations with the churches and over the collecting of direct taxation. Further concessions were made to the southern states to break down their resistance towards their incorporation in the Reich. Bavaria and

Wurttemberg retained their own postal and telegraph systems, and Bavaria kept control over its own army in peacetime. In making these concessions Bismarck was aware that they could weaken the unity of the Reich but he considered them to be a necessary compromise, especially as many of the concessions were of little more than symbolic value.

Prussian particularism

There was another, more powerful reason why Bismarck was prepared to make concessions to particularism. The King of Prussia, his army and civil service and the Junker aristocracy had no more desire to merge the state of Prussia within the Reich than did their counterparts in the south. In Bismarck's eyes, conservative Prussia was the backbone of the Reich; Prussia's monopoly of military power, its controlling position within the Bundestag, and the Prussian constitution which enabled the Junkers to dominate its political and administrative system, were a guarantee against any possibility of the Reich government giving in to the forces of liberalism and democracy. As long as the states retained power over their own local constitutions and important functions such as education and taxation, conservative domination in Prussia could protect the position of the Junker aristocracy.

The Reichstag

The Reichstag, in contrast to the Bundestag, symbolised the unity of the Reich. Elected by universal manhood suffrage, through national elections based on constituencies in every state and region of Germany, the Reichstag was the one truly national institution within the complex governmental structure of the Reich. Its ability to fulfil its role as a focus of national unity, however, was hampered by a number of factors. Firstly, the lack of genuine power over the accountability of ministers and over the initiation of legislation pushed the Reichstag into a position where opposition to the government was its only means of asserting itself. Conflict between the government and the Reichstag was a regular feature of the politics of the Second Reich and was increasing in intensity during the 1880s. This is not to say that many deputies were comfortable with placing themselves in opposition to the state. Many Germans and their parliamentary representatives from a wide spectrum of politics would have agreed with the influential historian Treitschke, who wrote that undeviating support for the state was the only correct way for a true German to behave in politics. Deputies from many parties were reluctant to challenge the political establishment and were unable to exercise their proper function of helping to determine the national interest. This role was assumed by Bismarck who did not hesitate to label any opposition which he encountered as unpatriotic and fractious.

The deputies

Secondly, the prestige of the Reichstag was diminished by the lack of ability on the part of the majority of deputies and by the unrepresentative nature of their social origins. The lower classes were effectively prevented from becoming deputies by the device of not paying them a salary. In the 1870s a high proportion of deputies came from the upper middle class and the landowners. Increasingly thereafter their places were filled by more professional politicians. Although there were some very able minds among the leaders of the political parties, the majority of the rank and file deputies had mediocre minds. They lacked the intellectual ability and the breadth of imagination to envisage a more positive role for themselves within the political life of the nation.

Political parties

Thirdly, political parties in the Reichstag represented sectional interests. Not one of the main political parties could claim to be a truly national party. The German Conservative party was the party of Prussianism, the aristocracy and the landed interest. Its main support came from the area east of the river Elbe. The Free Conservatives drew support from both landlords and industrialists. Neither of these two parties was ever in a position to command a majority in the Reichstag. The National Liberal party, which was the main supporter of unification in the late 1860s and of modernisation in the 1870s, drew its support from the wealthy middle class and higher officials. It was strong in Saxony, Hanover, Baden and the industrial areas of the Rhineland, but weak elsewhere. The Centre party represented Catholic interests and had support in the south, the Rhineland, Silesia and the Polish provinces. Of these parties, the National Liberals and the Centre had the broadest bases of support but the National Liberals were divided and in decline after 1879 and the Centre could only ever speak on behalf of one section of the German people. In the 1880s the fragmentation of politics grew worse as the socialist Social Democratic party (the SPD) attracted an increasing number of working-class votes and the middle-class vote was divided between the National Liberals and the Freisinnige party.

In these circumstances it is not surprising that many Germans saw the Reichstag as symbolising the conflict of interests and the antagonism between parties that were destructive of national unity. It was left to the executive to determine and to represent what were considered to be the true interests of the nation.

How far was the constitution based on the principles of liberalism and nationalism?

Concessions to 'popular will'. At first sight it seems clear that the constitution of the Second Reich owed little to the principles of liberalism and nationalism. Sovereignty within the Reich rested not with the

German people but with the princes, and the constitution was presented as a gift from above. Concessions to the 'popular will' appeared to have been made through the granting of the franchise to all adult males for elections to the Reichstag, but Bismarck made this gesture in the belief that the peasants could be trusted to vote for loyal and patriotic candidates. Bismarck frequently emphasised that the ultimate source of authority in the Reich was the Kaiser and, as his difficulties with the Reichstag mounted in the 1880s, he gave serious consideration to a coup d'état to reduce its powers – thus demonstrating that concessions which had been granted by royal favour can also be withdrawn.

Particularism versus nationalism. The constitution gave legal and institutional form to a united Germany, but the Reich was not a unitary state. The individual states retained considerable autonomy over important areas of policy such as education and justice and only the states could levy direct taxation. These concessions to particularism reveal how limited was nationalist influence in the framing of the constitution, yet it is important to recognise that there were also elements of the constitution which enshrined the unitary principle. The Reichstag was a national institution which, despite its limited powers, became the focal point of German politics. A share in legislative power and the right to review the budget gave political parties like the National Liberals the opportunity to influence government policy and to play their part in the shaping of the new Germany. With national unity achieved the authoritarian system had won the acceptance of the middle class and the National Liberal party had no wish to see greater democracy in Germany.

A compromise. The constitution of 1871 does not easily fit into conventional categories. It was a compromise between conservative particularism and the liberal desire for a more unitary state. Power rested with the princes but there were concessions to parliamentary rule and popular participation in government. Broadly speaking, this was a compromise which was acceptable to the overwhelming majority of Germans in the 1870s.

HOW SUCCESSFUL WAS BISMARCK IN PROMOTING UNITY?

As the man who was credited with being the architect of unification Bismarck occupied a unique position within the politics of the Reich. His own stature and prestige together with the uniquely powerful position he held within the government of the Reich were such that he was regarded by many Germans as personifying the political strength of the nation. He was, at one and the same time, the Reich Chancellor and the Minister-President of Prussia; as such he had the responsibility for reconciling Prussian particularism with the need to forge a national identity. His power derived from the fact that he had been appointed by the King of Prussia (who was also Kaiser of the German Reich) and was accountable to the monarch. But he was also the only minister who reported directly to the Reichstag and he needed the support of a majority of deputies in order to get his legislation passed. He had a delicate and difficult balancing act to perform if the whole system were not to implode under the strain of conflicting interests.

Bismarck as a moderniser

In some respects Bismarck showed considerable boldness and breadth of vision in the policies he pursued. His decision to allow the Reichstag to be elected on the basis of universal manhood suffrage was regarded, even by some of the National Liberals, as a dangerous experiment with democracy. Bismarck, however, believed that the majority of the lower classes, especially the peasants, would vote for conservative parties and that universal suffrage could consolidate the unity of the Reich. The masses, he believed, 'would stand on the side of kingship'. In the early years of the Reich's existence, also, he forged a working alliance with the National Liberal party to push through the work of modernising the country's institutions. In this way, a new national currency was introduced, the banking system modernised and the legal system reformed.

Bismarck as a conservative

In many other ways, however, Bismarck was part of the problem. Far from wishing to see Prussia and its institutions modernised, he resisted pressures for reform. The army was protected from parliamentary control and interference by the Septennial Law of 1874. There was no reform of the conservative Prussian constitution which protected the political power of the Junker class. As the Reichstag became increasingly unmanageable in the 1880s Bismarck fell back more and more on the conservative bastion of Prussia to maintain the Reich on the basis on which it had been created in 1871. A thorough purge was undertaken in the civil service to remove any high officials with liberal views. Army officers who supported opposition parties were forced to resign their commissions. The loyalty of the army was of particular importance; as an official directive of the 1880s put it, the army was 'the only fixed point in the whirlpool, the rock in the sea of revolution that threatens us on all sides'. In the eyes of Bismarck and the ruling elite a purified army and civil service were essential props to the power of the Prussian monarchy. That these policies were also divisive is shown by the growth of anti-militaristic attitudes, especially among the opposition parties.

Bismarck's temperament

Bismarck's own temperament also contributed to the atmosphere of conflict. He was intolerant of opposition; in his eyes the government was always right and parliamentary opposition was motivated by selfish and narrow interests. Co-operation with parties in the Reichstag in order to secure majorities for his policies was merely an expedient. Political alliances could change as the situation demanded. Bismarck could also be very excitable, quick to identify conspiracies against the state and liable to over-react. His decision to launch the Kulturkampf and his anti-socialist campaign after 1879 display some of these characteristics. In both cases Bismarck pursued highly divisive policies in the cause of defending the unity of the Reich against what were, in his eyes, *Reichsfeinde* (enemies of the Reich) Neither campaign was successful in suppressing the so-called Reichsfeinde and in both cases the divisions in German society were exacerbated by the heavy-handed attempts at repression.

The significance of the Kulturkampf

For Bismarck the main factor in his decision to begin a divisive attack on the Catholic church so early in the history of the Reich was his belief that the Centre party represented a threat to the unity of the Reich. The Centre had become a rallying point for south-German Catholics, Poles, Danes, the recently annexed population of Alsace–Lorraine and the supporters of the deposed Guelf dynasty of Hanover. The Centre opposed policies which would create a more centralised Reich and championed the interests of the separate states. Thus the Centre party could legitimately be regarded as undermining the unity of the Reich; but the *Kulturkampf* was even more divisive in its effects. The campaign deliberately set Catholic against Protestant and encouraged the Catholic minority to feel alienated from the Reich. The application of the campaign in Poland also strengthened Polish nationalism and led to the growth of Polish peasant organisations which attempted to preserve their national culture and prevent the ejection of Polish peasants from their farms. According to **Williamson** (1986), many modern German historians see the Kulturkampf as a classic example of Bismarck's technique of 'negative integration', whereby the majority Protestant part of the population would be united in the face of an apparent threat from the Roman Catholic church. If this were the intention then even on this level it was less than successful since the Kulturkampf, by its severity and blatant discrimination, alienated many Protestants as well.

The Kulturkampf and its effects on the National Liberal party. The Kulturkampf was also significant in the relationship between Bismarck and the National Liberals. Although the decision to launch the campaign was Bismarck's alone he was enthusiastically supported and encouraged in this by the National Liberal party. Whereas Bismarck was motivated primarily by political considerations, for the National Liberals there were ideological issues at stake as well. Liberals in all European countries at this time viewed the Roman Catholic church as an enemy of progress and greater individual freedom: the recent decrees from Pope Pius IX on the Syllabus of Errors and the Doctrine of Papal Infallibility reinforced liberal

objections to Catholicism. In Germany, the establishment of a new Catholic political party, the Centre, was viewed by the National Liberals as a sign of Catholic determination not merely to protect their influence in German society but also to extend it. The National Liberals thus proved useful allies for Bismarck when he decided to launch the attack on the Catholic church.

The end of the Kulturkampf and the decline of The National Liberal party.
The decision to begin the process of ending the Kulturkampf was also made by Bismarck. Here again he was motivated primarily by political factors. The Centre party, far from being damaged by the campaign, had in fact gained in strength as Catholics rallied in defence of their church. In 1874 the Centre party had doubled its vote in the Reichstag elections and had emerged as a significant force in German politics. The National Liberals, on the other hand, were severely damaged by the Kulturkampf. In the cause of defending freedom they had supported the introduction of new laws which denied religious freedom to a large section of German society and placed themselves firmly on the side of an authoritarian state. This betrayal of their own philosophy was one of the factors which undermined the confidence and morale of the party and brought about its decline. Bismarck was beginning to find his relationship with the National Liberals increasingly irksome, especially when he offered its leader, Bennigsen, a post in government and the party demanded two more posts. This was more than Bismarck was prepared to concede. Bismarck was also, in 1878, shifting his economic policy towards the reintroduction of tariffs, a policy which the National Liberals would have difficulty in supporting whereas the Centre party might prove to be useful allies.

When the Kulturkampf was begun the National Liberals were the largest party in the Reichstag and, through their alliance with Bismarck, they were able to exercise some influence over government policy. By 1878, when Bismarck had decided to abandon the Kulturkampf and undertake tariff reform, the National Liberal party was in decline and on the defensive. The National Liberals suffered from the effects of the economic depression of 1873 which undermined support for their laissez-faire and free trade policies but they also suffered severe damage from their identification with the deeply flawed and unsuccessful attempt to suppress the Catholic church. It is ironic that a party which, more than any other in German politics, stood for greater individual freedom and national unity, should throw itself with such enthusiasm into a campaign which damaged both of these causes; in the process the National Liberal party contributed to its own steep decline.

HOW DID SOCIAL AND ECONOMIC CHANGE AFFECT THE COHESION OF THE GERMAN REICH?

Industrialisation

Between 1871 and 1890 the German Reich underwent rapid and far-reaching social and economic change. These changes were described in Chapter 9. The depression and financial crisis of 1873 dealt a severe blow to the confidence of German farmers and many industrialists and changed the whole context of political debate in the Reich in the years following. Despite this setback to industrial enterprise the industrial sector of the economy continued to grow over the next twenty years and Germany emerged as one of the world's leading producers of manufactured goods. Industrialisation brought in its train a shift in population from the countryside to the growing towns and cities and fundamental changes in the class structure of society. The middle class grew in numbers and began to outstrip the aristocracy in terms of personal wealth. The industrial areas also witnessed the growth of a working class most of whom experienced the typical problems of a society in the early stages of industrialisation. Poor working conditions, long hours, low wages and unhealthy living conditions were the norm for large numbers of coal miners and factory workers; growing discontent was the result. The sharpening of class tensions was reflected in the growing trade union movement and in the increasing number of strikes in the late 1880s.

Social changes in the cities

In the cities the traditional hierarchical structure of society was breaking down. Workers who left country villages to seek employment in the cities left behind a society based on a rigid hierarchy in which the peasants deferred to their social superiors – the landowner and the pastor (or priest) – for direction in all matters, including political allegiance. In the cities the relationship between employer and employee was, with some notable exceptions such as the Krupp enterprises in Essen, purely an economic one. Most employers accepted no obligation to safeguard the welfare of their employees and their workers were not in the habit of accepting political or social guidance from their bosses.

Workers who migrated from countryside to town also tended to leave their habit of church going behind them and the churches began to experience a decline in attendance as a result of these social and economic changes. Within the Catholic church there were some, such as the Bishop of Mainz, who tried to respond to this challenge. The Bishop believed that the church had a duty to help the working class to withstand the demoralising effects of industrialisation by organising co-operative societies, Christian trade unions and recreational clubs. The Centre party also championed the cause of social reform. The Evangelical church, with its close links to the Prussian state, was socially more conservative although it did carry out mission work in the cities in an attempt to maintain its congregations.

The education system

The education system did not provide a means of escape from the poverty and degradation of working-class life in the cities. Germany had the most developed state system of elementary education of any country in Europe. Due to the establishment of state elementary schools in most German states in the 18th century, Germany had the highest rate of literacy in Europe; its economic success was partly due to this. Many Prussian conservatives feared that the education of the children of peasants and workers would be subversive of the hierarchical social structure, but, in fact, the school system reinforced it. In elementary schools the emphasis of teaching was on order and discipline and obedience to authority. The inclusion of history in the curriculum after 1870 was designed to nurture 'nationalistic young Germans' by concentrating on the glories of recent German history. The organisation of the school system did not encourage or facilitate upward social mobility. Only an elementary education was available to the children of the peasants and the working class. Secondary education, which was the route to higher qualifications and social advancement, was far too expensive for working-class families. **Craig** (1981) has written that the education system was 'structured in a way that effectively kept the masses in their place'.

The rise of the Social Democratic party (SPD) – the Socialist party

Social and economic change added to the tensions and conflicts in German society. Despite the efforts of the churches and the availability of education, the conflicts grew in intensity, particularly during the 1880s. This was reflected in the rise of the Socialist party, which was regarded by Germany's rulers as the greatest threat to the unity and cohesion of the Reich that they had so far encountered. Bismarck after 1879 became increasingly obsessed with the apparent threat posed by the SPD as the party continued to gain in strength despite his efforts to suppress it. The rise of the SPD with its revolutionary philosophy undermined many of the assumptions on which the 1871 constitution had been based, especially the idea that the masses could be relied upon to support the monarchy. The presence of a sizeable group of deputies in the Reichstag who demanded greater democracy and parliamentary control over the executive greatly exacerbated the inherent contradiction in Bismarck's constitution between monarchical power and parliamentary rule. It was a conflict that could not be resolved by Bismarck's usual techniques of threats and concessions. The way in which Germany's rulers dealt with the SPD, therefore, was the main test of how well they coped with the consequences of social and economic change.

HOW DID GERMANY'S RULERS COPE WITH THE CONSEQUENCES OF SOCIAL AND ECONOMIC CHANGE?

Economic depression

The economic depression which began in 1873 and the rapid social and economic change of the 1880s changed the context of German politics. According to **Craig** (1981), 'the fundamental weakness of the (German) political system was its social immobility. Bismarck assumed that the balance between the democratic–constitutional and the aristocratic–monarchical forces would remain basically unchanged and that he could continue standing between the two camps, making the adjustments necessary to keep the system working.' The threat to the livelihoods and social standing of the landowners which was posed by the depression, followed by the rise in the Social Democratic party which was a consequence of social and economic change, rendered Bismarck's assumptions untenable. The response of the government to these problems had far-reaching consequences for the internal unity and cohesion of the Reich.

Tariff reform

The return to trade protection in 1879 was the immediate response to the depression. In some ways the introduction of protective tariffs gave a new lease of life to the Reich. The work of unification was consolidated by the renewed emphasis for farmers and manufacturers on catering for a large internal market. Agricultural producers all over Germany, not just on the Junker estates to the east, benefited from the protection against imports, as did manufacturers. One of the results of trade protection, therefore, was to accelerate the trend for the middle class to identify more closely with the aristocracy – the so-called 'alliance of steel and rye' referred to in Chapter 8. On the other hand, protective tariffs led to generally higher prices, especially for basic foodstuffs such as bread. This, in turn, led to a lowering of working-class living standards and added to growing class tensions.

Political reform

Once the constitution of 1871 had been introduced no provision was made to keep it under review. In the context of a society which was undergoing rapid social and economic change and in which the context of political debate was shifting, this was a serious omission. The Reichstag elections of the 1880s were still conducted on the basis of the electoral boundaries drawn up in 1871, despite the fact that there had been significant changes in the distribution of the population. The result was that the Reichstag became increasingly unrepresentative.

Restatement of the Kaiser's power. Few attempts were made by Bismarck to reform the system of government, despite the growing pressure for change. Such changes as were made were intended to strengthen monarchical power. In 1882, for example, a royal decree reiterated the position that the Kaiser was personally responsible for the direction of his government's policy and that civil servants were bound by their oath of loyalty to the monarch to support that policy. Although primarily of symbolic importance this decree was, nevertheless, a reminder to the increasingly fractious Reichstag that royal power was a permanent reality.

Loss of political control over the army. Of more importance was the loss of political control over the army in 1883. The Military Cabinet and the army General Staff were no longer subject to the authority of the War Minister but were to report directly to the Kaiser. Like the Septennial Law of 1874 this measure was designed to protect the army from political interference, a defensive response to the problem of an increasingly unmanageable Reichstag. Bismarck, who had always striven to assert the primacy of the civil power over that of the military, was to learn to his cost that giving the army political independence not only weakened the powers of the Reichstag but was also a threat to his own position. During the 1887 Bulgarian crisis, for example, the General Staff began to interfere in the framing of German foreign policy. Although Bismarck was able to reassert his own authority on this occasion, he had bequeathed to his successors a position which severely undermined their ability to control the army and prevent the General Staff from interfering in foreign policy.

Politics in the 1880s

German political life was very different after the tariff reform debate of 1878–9. In the early years of the Reich Bismarck had leaned very heavily on the National Liberal party to push his modernising legislation through the Reichstag. For all its weaknesses and its faults the National Liberal party was the one party capable of commanding sufficient votes to secure a workable majority in the Reichstag and was one of the few parties with a truly national agenda. The party was beginning to decline, however, and the tariff reform issue accelerated this process by causing the party to split. German politics in the 1880s became increasingly fragmented as political parties came to represent narrow, sectional economic interests rather than attempting to command more broadly based support.

The anti-socialist campaign

The Anti-Socialist Law of 1878 and its rigorous enforcement in the years to 1890 were another response of the government to the consequences of social and economic change. The emergence of the SPD and its subsequent rapid growth into a major political party were regarded by Bismarck as a major threat to the survival of the Reich. Socialists were treated as Reichsfeinde since their advocacy of revolution to overturn an autocratic monarchy and their support for socialist internationalism meant that they could not be 'good Germans'. Official government policy through the 1880s was increasingly obsessed with countering 'socialist subversion'; opposition from whatever political direction was treated with growing suspicion and vigorous efforts were made to purge the civil service, the army and the education system of any disloyal elements. In short, the almost hysterical reaction to the rise of socialism poisoned German political life and divided German society even more. Working-class followers of the SPD felt stigmatised and excluded from society. The movement was driven underground and developed its own 'alternative culture' in order to withstand the assault. The divisive effects of the Anti-Socialist Law were partly mitigated by the introduction of social welfare benefits – the so-called 'state socialism' – which gave ordinary working-class Germans a stake in society. The fact remained, however, that, in the cause of defending the Reich and upholding German patriotic values, the government only succeeded in exacerbating the growing class tensions in German society.

Sammlungspolitik

Bismarck's other response to the growth in opposition which was a consequence of social and economic change was to attempt to create a parliamentary coalition, or *Sammlung*, that would unite around a right-wing political agenda and form a solid block in the Reichstag. The Conservative party, Free Conservative party and the rump of the National Liberal party formed the nucleus of this coalition but, only in 1887 when the three parties formed the Kartell, did they secure a working majority in the Reichstag. For the rest of the time the support of at least part of the Centre party was necessary to achieve a majority although, with some of the anti-Catholic laws still in force until 1887, the Centre party could not be relied upon.

The result was that Bismarck had increasing difficulty in managing the Reichstag in the 1880s. His success in 1887 was largely because the election was held in an atmosphere of national danger which was deliberately contrived by Bismarck to appeal to the patriotism of the voters. The success of the Kartell, however, was short-lived as it broke up in 1890 and Bismarck was faced yet again with a recalcitrant opposition in the Reichstag. At the end of his career he gave serious consideration to a coup d'état to restrict the franchise, remove many of the Reichstag's powers and make the constitution even more autocratic. This was a sign of Bismarck's desperation and is evidence of the extent to which the political system of Germany was failing to adapt to the social and economic changes in German society.

CONCLUSION

Class divisions, religious differences and regional variations were not unique to Germany. Conflicts between traditional forces and those pressing for the modernisation of society are common features of any society undergoing rapid political, social and economic change as was Germany during the years 1871–90. It is also not surprising that German society exhibited conflicts between those groups who benefited as a result of economic change and those who considered themselves to be its victims. What, perhaps, made these divisions wider and the resulting conflicts more bitter in Germany than in other comparable societies was the stubborn determination of the conservative aristocratic and monarchical forces to protect their position in the face of demands to reform and their inability to adapt to the new social and economic realities. The ruling elite showed an increasing nervousness about threats to their position, both apparent and real, and fell back on the conservative bastions of the Prussian constitution, the Prussian army and the autocratic powers of the monarchy to defend a traditional way of life.

The anti-socialist campaign became the main focus of this struggle. That the campaign was an overreaction is a view which is now generally accepted by historians, who point to the development of the SPD after 1890 into a reformist, constitutional party. Bismarck acted without the benefit of hindsight but even he was aware of the deep reservoir of patriotism among Germans of all classes which could be tapped to enlist support for the government. It was an appeal to patriotism in the face of an apparent external threat which served Bismarck so well in 1887. What Bismarck was unable and unwilling to do, however, was to build a consensus on the basis of compromise with the democratic–constitutional forces. Continuing conflict was the inevitable result.

SECTION 4

How successful was German foreign policy, 1871–90?

KEY POINTS

An assessment of the success of German policy in the first nineteen years of the Second Reich needs to be based on three criteria.

- Did the foreign policy promote the basic external and internal interests of the Reich?
- Was that foreign policy applied consistently?
- Was Germany's position in relation to the other powers stronger or weaker in 1890 than it had been in 1871?

INTRODUCTION

The German Reich had been created through a series of wars in the years 1864–71. Bismarck had shown himself to be adept at exploiting the opportunities which were available to Prussia and temperamentally well-suited to employing the aggressive diplomacy which wrong-footed Austria and France. The situation after 1871 was very different and the foreign policy priorities of the German Reich would have to be different also. How successful was Bismarck in adapting his foreign policy to the changed circumstances and how well did he promote the external interests of the Reich in the period 1871–90?

WHAT WERE THE BASIC AIMS OF GERMAN FOREIGN POLICY?

A 'satiated power'

In surveying the European scene in1871 after the creation of the German Reich, Bismarck was conscious of both the strengths and weaknesses of Germany's position. The Prussian army had achieved victories over two of Europe's greatest powers; the population of the new Reich was larger than that of France; and Germany was experiencing rapid economic growth. But this very success made Germany vulnerable because, as the history of Europe has shown, any power which has threatened to dominate the continent has become the target of a hostile European coalition. Any further expansion by Germany, therefore, was liable to provoke a hostile coalition. Bismarck's first priority was to consolidate the gains Germany had made. 'When we have arrived in a good harbour', he said, 'we should be content, and cultivate and hold what we have won.'

French isolation

The second main objective was to ensure that France should remain isolated, since without allies it was unlikely that the French desire for *revanche* (revenge) would result in a French attack on Germany. French hostility to Germany after 1871 was a 'negative constant' in Bismarck's foreign policy calculations. He, therefore, worked for an 'overall political situation in which all powers except France have need of us and are, as far as possible, kept from forming coalitions against us'. He also worked to ensure that, should alliances be formed, Germany should be part of the largest grouping. 'All politics reduce themselves', he once wrote, 'to this formula; to try to be one of three, as long as the world is governed by an unstable equilibrium of five powers.'

Peace

Thirdly, it was in Germany's interests to remain at peace with its neighbours and to try to ensure that they remained at peace with each other. 'The task of our policy', said Bismarck, 'is, if possible to prevent war entirely and, if that is not possible, at least to postpone it.' Other powers, particularly France, were not entirely convinced of Germany's peaceful intentions, particularly when Bismarck engaged in some crude sabre-rattling during the 'War in Sight' crisis of 1875. Bismarck certainly would not rule out the possibility of war at some future date and the peace he desired was one on Germany's terms. But Bismarck was acutely aware of the danger that a European war, even one which did not initially involve Germany and which did not threaten its vital interests, might nevertheless widen into a more general conflict from which no great power could stand aside. In such a circumstance the tension between France and Germany would add an additional dimension to the conflict and France would have less difficulty in finding allies.

Domestic political pressures

Finally, it is important to acknowledge that foreign policy did not operate within a political vacuum. Although foreign policy was primarily concerned with relations between Germany and the other powers, domestic political considerations were an important factor in determining its priorities and its application. Indeed, some historians have argued that domestic considerations were the prime factor in determining foreign policy. Bismarck, in 1871, was aware of the fragile nature of the new Reich and his priority was to strengthen its internal cohesion. His desire for external peace coincided with the need for internal consolidation. Foreign policy decisions had to be based on calculations as to how they would affect interest groups in Germany, how they would be received by the electorate and how they would relate to domestic policy objectives. In the final analysis, however, it was strategic considerations which were paramount when Bismarck made decisions about foreign policy.

HOW EFFECTIVELY WERE THESE AIMS PURSUED IN BISMARCK'S FOREIGN POLICY?

Overview

Bismarck was an arch-pragmatist who was very flexible in his dealings with foreign powers. At first sight his foreign policy between 1871 and 1890 appears to be a series of twists and turns. This is particularly true of his dealings with France and Russia. Although he took French hostility for granted and built his policy around the need to isolate the French, there was a period in Franco-German relations between 1879 and about 1885 when relations between the two powers were relatively cordial. Similarly, in his dealings with Russia, he played a game of brinkmanship throughout the 1870s and 1880s. His dealings with Russia were characterised by the use of threats – the Dual Alliance with Austria–Hungary was partly designed to put pressure on Russia – whilst simultaneously Bismarck was trying to tie the Russians into a loose relationship with Germany. All of these twists and turns, however, were tactical shifts. Bismarck was reacting to events as they occurred. Alliances, military commitments, threats, bilateral and multilateral deals with other powers were all employed at various times as Bismarck tried to apply the approach which had served him so well in the years 1862–71: the 'strategy of alternatives'. His objectives were the same in 1890 as they had been in 1871, but his methods were infinitely flexible, so flexible in fact that only Bismarck himself could understand the complexities of the policy he had developed.

Turning points. Within this overall pattern of flexibility, however, there were some significant turning points. The first of these was in 1871 when Bismarck's foreign policy goals changed. In the process of unification Prussia's policy was one of expansion and this was pursued through an essentially aggressive approach to Austria and then to France. After 1871 the priority was consolidation and peace. In 1875, however, Bismarck again attempted to use aggressive tactics to put pressure on France in the 'War in Sight' crisis. This resulted in a serious diplomatic defeat for Bismarck as it alarmed the other powers; Great Britain and Russia put pressure on Germany to desist from its threats. The failure of his tactics on this occasion caused Bismarck to be more circumspect in his dealings with other powers in the future.

The events of 1878–9 mark an important turning point in German foreign policy, just as there were important changes in the German domestic political scene. The main foreign policy change was the decision to enter into a permanent military alliance with Austria–Hungary. Although the German Reich and the Austro-Hungarian Empire had been linked since 1873 through the *Dreikaiserbund*, that was an entirely different kind of relationship. Where the Dreikaiserbund had involved no firm commitments by any of the powers and was a three-sided arrangement, the Dual Alliance involved a firm commitment by Germany to support Austria–Hungary in a war with Russia and was a permanent arrangement. Thus Bismarck had sacrificed much of the flexibility which was a key feature of his diplomacy in return for a permanent ally. However, in that alliance Austria–Hungary refused to give Germany the same guarantee of support against France as Germany had given to Austria–Hungary against Russia. In the short term the drawbacks in the Dual Alliance were not a major concern to Bismarck because he was able to use his diplomatic skills to maintain a working relationship with Russia and to keep France isolated, but in the longer term his successors found their freedom of action in foreign policy restricted by the Dual Alliance.

Bismarck's alliance system. The Dual Alliance with Austria–Hungary was followed over the course of the next ten years by alliances with Italy (1882), Romania (1883), the Three Emperors' Alliance (1881) and the Reinsurance Treaty with Russia (1887). In 1887 also there were the Mediterranean Agreements between Great Britain, Austria–Hungary and Italy which were an attempt to contain French, and later Russian, ambitions in the Mediterranean and the Near East. Although these agreements did not directly involve Germany, the fact that its allies were linked to Great Britain gave Germany also an indirect link. This intricate and complex series of agreements and alliances had the effect of denying the French any potential allies and allowed Bismarck, who was the only statesman even in Germany to understand the logic behind them, to retain the diplomatic initiative. **Craig** (1981) has written that in the years 1879–82, when many of these agreements were being concluded, Bismarck 'moved with assurance and aplomb, taking advantage of the apprehensions of the other governments, making the most of the unforeseen opportunities, always retaining the initiative and by 1882 he had so enhanced Germany's position that Berlin was regarded as the diplomatic capital of Europe'.

In many ways Bismarck retained the initiative and continued to devise further diplomatic expedients to keep abreast of the changing situation in Europe during the remainder of his period in office. How far these agreements were sustainable in the long term however is open to question, particularly as they began to unravel quite soon after his departure in 1890. It is also questionable whether Bismarck always made the most of the opportunities open to him and whether he was wise to enter into the commitments that he made. This question is best approached by studying Germany's relations with each of the other main powers in turn.

Relations with France

It has already been stated that French hostility to the new German Reich and their desire for a future war of revenge was taken to be a 'negative constant' in Germany's foreign policy. It suited German interests, therefore, that France should remain diplomatically isolated and politically weak. The early years of the new French Third Republic brought weak and unstable governments which posed no threat to Germany and which were unlikely to attract any other powers to conclude an alliance with France. When the French economy recovered from the effects of the war more quickly than Bismarck had thought possible, the French government paid off the indemnity to Germany and the German occupying army had to be withdrawn. This was the background to the 'War in Sight' crisis which resulted in a diplomatic defeat for Bismarck.

Franco-German co-operation. From 1877 the French Republic was led by moderate governments which concentrated more on internal affairs and the expansion of the French overseas empire and therefore pushed *revanchisme* into the background. Bismarck responded to this change of circumstance by adopting a more conciliatory policy towards France. One key element in this approach was to encourage the French to expand their empire in Africa. This would have two potential advantages for Germany. Firstly, as he himself told the French Ambassador in 1878, it would 'turn your eyes away from Alsace–Lorraine'. Secondly, it would bring the French into conflict with other powers which had ambitions in that region, particularly Great Britain and Italy. Thus, Bismarck supported the French in the dispute with Britain over Egypt and in the dispute with Italy over Tunis, expressing himself as being delighted to see the French 'scattering their energies in new areas while picking up new enemies on the way'.

By 1884, when Germany entered the 'scramble for Africa', relations with France were relatively cordial and the two powers were able to co-operate in this sphere. A common rivalry with Great Britain thus became the basis for close co-operation between them in preparing the ground for the Berlin Conference of 1885 which regulated the competition between the powers over the Congo region of Africa. Shared interests in the colonial sphere, however, were no basis for long-term co-operation and no foundation for Germany's security. The defeat of the moderate republicans in the French elections brought a more aggressively nationalistic government to power in France in 1886. The appointment of **General Boulanger** as French War Minister changed the atmosphere between the two powers since Boulanger was renowned for his anti-

KEY PERSON

General Boulanger
Boulanger was a French general who became Minister of War in 1886; he dominated French politics in the next three years. His radical rhetoric and patriotic attacks on Germany won him popular support. His rapid rise to power threw the French Third Republic into crisis as he was suspected of having ambitions to become a new Napoleon. The crisis passed when he lost his nerve and fled into exile.

HEINEMANN ADVANCED HISTORY

German sentiments. Bismarck exploited the rise of Boulanger to generate an atmosphere of crisis in Germany, a device that produced gains for the pro-government Kartell parties in the general election of 1887. Although Boulanger was dropped from the French cabinet in 1887 relations between France and Germany remained cool thereafter.

In his dealings with France Bismarck showed flexibility and pragmatism. Although not all of his dealings with France were successful, his main objective of keeping France isolated was achieved. He was able to exploit French ambitions in Africa to help drive a wedge between France and Britain, but this was merely a short-term expedient which did not provide a firm foundation for long-term German security.

Relations with Russia

'The secret of politics', wrote Bismarck in 1863, 'is a good treaty with Russia.' He saw Russia, because of its size and geographical position, as the pivot of the European diplomatic system and placed great emphasis on maintaining a good working relationship with the government of the Tsar. It was in Germany's interests that Russia should not make an alliance with France since this would face Germany with the prospect of a war on two fronts. It was also in Germany's interests that Russia and Austria should not go to war over their increasingly conflicting interests in the Balkans. Any war between two major European powers would be likely to escalate into a wider conflict from which it would be difficult for Germany to stand aside. Such a war would give France the opportunity to intervene and break out of its isolation. Thus the three-sided Dreikaiserbund of 1873 seemed to provide the ideal solution to these problems, especially as it involved no firm commitment by Germany to either power. It protected Germany from the dangers of isolation at minimum cost to Germany.

Difficulties affecting Russo-German relations. The Congress of Berlin in 1878 and the Dual Alliance of 1879 mark something of a turning point in Germany's relations with Russia. Russian anger towards Germany over the outcome of the Congress combined with other factors to put Russo-German relations under severe strain. Trade relations were a source of friction. German exports of manufactured goods were harmed by the introduction of tariffs by Russia in 1877 and Russia's exports of grain were severely affected by the introduction of the German tariff in 1879. There was great personal animosity between Bismarck and the Russian Foreign Secretary, Gorchakov. After 1881, with the accession of a new and inexperienced Tsar, Alexander III, a sound working relationship between Germany and Russia became increasingly difficult to maintain. The Tsar received conflicting advice from rival groups of advisers and tried to implement both points of view in his foreign policy, which became as a result inconsistent and unstable.

From 1879, also, Germany was linked to Austria–Hungary through the Dual Alliance. In a situation of growing rivalry between Austria–Hungary and Russia over the Balkans, a firm and permanent alliance between Austria–Hungary and Germany was bound to place a strain on relations between Russia and Germany. Indeed, it was part of Bismarck's thinking when concluding the Dual Alliance that it would be a useful device for putting pressure on Russia to desist from aggressive moves in the Balkans and to seek an accommodation with Germany. In the short term, Bismarck's calculations proved correct. The Three Emperors' Alliance of 1881 was a stop-gap measure to keep a link between Germany and Russia and to try to manage the conflict between Russia and Austria–Hungary. This Alliance could not, however, lead to a stable Russo-German friendship. Conflict between Russia and Austria–Hungary was bound to recur at some stage, as happened in the years 1885–7 when the Bulgarian crisis flared up again, and when it did Russia and Germany would have interests which diverged.

The Bulgarian crisis, 1885–7. The Bulgarian crisis provides useful insights into the state of Russo-German relations towards the end of Bismarck's period in office. Russia and Austria–Hungary viewed each other with increasing suspicion and hostility as the crisis developed. Both looked to Germany for support. Bismarck manoeuvred desperately to maintain a link with Russia whilst at the same time strengthening Austria–Hungary. Thus the Reinsurance Treaty with Russia was a response to the first of these needs and one which, moreover, appeared to contradict the second. Considerable concessions were made by Bismarck, including the commitment to support Russia in Bulgaria – a concession which was directly in conflict with the spirit of the Dual Alliance. At the same time Bismarck sought to put pressure on Russia through his sponsorship of the Mediterranean Agreements and through his decision to block the efforts of the Russian government to raise a loan from German banks. These moves did have the effect of restraining Russia in Bulgaria, and in this way European peace was preserved. After the most serious threat to European peace since 1878, the Dual Alliance was still intact and Russia was still linked to Germany through a formal treaty. On the other hand, Russo-German relations had come under severe strain and the decision to block a German loan to Russia had forced the Tsar to turn to the French money market to secure the finance needed.

Relations between Germany and Russia were placed under severe strain after 1878 and Bismarck's responses to the problem were a series of short-term expedients. With the benefit of hindsight we can see that the attempt to maintain a co-operative relationship with both Austria–Hungary and Russia *and* keep France and Russia apart was unsustainable. Within three years of Bismarck's departure an alliance was to be concluded between Russia and France and Bismarck's policy was in ruins. When he left office in 1890, however, the Reinsurance Treaty with Russia was nearing the end of its three-year term and not only Bismarck but the Russian government also were keen to renew it. Thus, despite the growing tensions and increasing suspicion on both sides, there was still some life left in Bismarck's policy of keeping open the link with Russia.

Relations with Austria–Hungary

After the victory at Koniggratz in 1866 Bismarck used all his influence to prevent the generals and the King from pressing on with the war and occupying Vienna. In the short term the priority was to end the war quickly and avoid any outside intervention, but there was also a long-term interest at stake. To continue the war and inflict more damage on Austria would run the risk of encouraging nationalist movements within the various provinces of the Austrian Empire and might start a chain reaction leading to its disintegration and collapse. Prussia's dispute with Austria was solely about which power should dominate Germany. Prussia had no interest in destroying the Austrian Empire completely. Indeed, such an outcome would destroy the delicate balance of power within Europe and lead to incalculable consequences. Therefore a quick end to the war was in Prussia's long-term interests as well.

The way the war was ended enabled a reconciliation between Germany and Austria much earlier than might otherwise have occurred. This reconciliation was also made possible by developments within Austria itself. In the wake of defeats in Italy and Germany the Austrian Empire was reorganised in 1867: it become the Austro-Hungarian Empire, and the centre of gravity of the new Empire shifted away from Germany and towards the Balkans. There were no longer any conflicts of interest between the two powers and a new relationship based on co-operation was possible.

The Dual Alliance. In the early 1870s Bismarck preferred to establish a relationship which was essentially symbolic – the Dreikaiserbund – and one which enabled Germany to maintain a position of equidistance between Russia and Austria–Hungary. After 1878, however, Bismarck became convinced that a much closer relationship with Austria–Hungary was essential in order to stabilise the Balkans, prevent Germany's isolation and put pressure on Russia. The result was the Dual Alliance. How far the Dual Alliance secured Bismarck's objectives, however, is open to debate. Bismarck had wanted to keep the terms of the Dual Alliance as general as possible to avoid Germany entering into specific commitments which would tie the hands of German diplomats in future. Instead he had to agree to Austria's demand for support against Russia. This concession was not balanced by any corresponding commitment by Austria–Hungary to support Germany against France. In these respects the Dual Alliance was more favourable to Austria–Hungary than to Germany.

The Dual Alliance became a cornerstone of German foreign policy throughout the remainder of Bismarck's term of office. For Bismarck the Dual Alliance was strictly defensive in purpose and in no way prevented him from entering into arrangements with other powers. He also believed that the Dual Alliance gave Germany greater influence with Austria–Hungary than would have been the case with a looser arrangement. He was careful not to give Austria–Hungary unconditional support – for example during the Bulgarian crisis of 1885–7 – since he wished to restrain the Austrians from provoking a war with Russia. He was also careful not to place too much reliance on the Dual Alliance to protect Germany's interests, especially in view of his lack of faith in Austrian military efficiency. For Bismarck the Dual Alliance was part of a much larger network of alliances and agreements which were all designed to keep France isolated and prevent a war. In this respect the Dual Alliance was a success but, in entering into a permanent arrangement with another power, Bismarck had limited his own, and his successors', freedom of manoeuvre.

Relations with Great Britain

Great Britain and Germany occupied separate spheres in the European balance of power. Where Germany was a continental power with a large army, Britain was a world power with a very large navy and an extensive overseas empire. Although there was growing trade rivalry between them, there were no conflicts of vital interests which would get in the way of co-operation between Britain and Germany. Yet, for most of the period 1871–90, both powers tended to keep each other at arm's length and there was little constructive engagement between them. Partly this was because of the British preference for not entering into commitments towards European powers and partly this was because, without a large army, Britain could not easily influence the outcome of events on the continent. British naval power could be brought to bear on some areas of Europe, however, as was the case when Britain intervened to force the Russians to revise the Treaty of Unkiar Skelessi in 1878. With a strong naval presence in the Mediterranean, Britain was an important counterweight to Russian expansion in the Balkans; British policy was normally, therefore, close to that of Austria–Hungary. The fact that Bismarck ignored Britain for much of the time and deliberately picked a quarrel with Britain over colonial expansion in Africa for a brief period in the 1880s has been criticised by some historians as a missed opportunity.

German domestic politics. Part of the explanation for this lies in the German domestic political situation. Bismarck was determined not to allow German politics to develop along British lines where the monarch had conceded real power to Parliament and ministers were constrained by the need to keep parliamentary majorities. The Crown Prince, Friedrich, was known to admire the British system and had married an English princess. Picking a quarrel with Britain was a way of emphasising the differences between the German system and the British and of undermining support for the Crown Prince and his policies. A dispute with Britain over colonies after 1884 also helped promote the growing co-operation with France at that time. Thus Bismarck supported France in the dispute with Britain over Egypt, and Germany's colonial acquisitions in Africa were in many cases a direct challenge to previously established British interests. For example, the German acquisition of South-West Africa was regarded as a threat by the British who were already established in South Africa and wished to expand northwards.

Closer relations with Great Britain. By 1887 the whole context of Anglo-German relations had changed. Bismarck had become disenchanted with the results of German colonial expansion and had no wish for further acquisitions. The era of co-operation with France was over and there was a serious crisis in the Balkans. Co-operation with Britain now seemed more attractive, especially as the British policy of restraining Russian expansion coincided with the German interest in preventing a war over Bulgaria. The result of these changes was the start of indirect co-operation with Britain through the two Mediterranean Agreements of 1887. Both agreements involved Britain, Austria–Hungary and Italy; the first was designed to restrain France and the second to restrain Russia by all three powers agreeing to work together to maintain the status quo in the Mediterranean and Balkan regions. The agreements were useful to Germany – which was why Bismarck helped to sponsor them – because they strengthened the Triple Alliance and kept France away from another potential ally. Moreover, this had been achieved at minimal cost to Germany. The Mediterranean Agreements were, like the Reinsurance Treaty with Russia, very short-lived however, and in the 1890s British and German interests began to diverge once again.

CONCLUSION

When Bismarck left office in 1890 Germany had experienced nineteen years of peace. By exploiting and encouraging the rivalries between the powers Bismarck had prevented the creation of a hostile coalition against Germany, and France was still isolated. It was a considerable achievement that, despite the growing rivalry between Austria–Hungary and Russia, Bismarck had succeeded in maintaining a working relationship with both powers and that Russia was still keen to renew the Reinsurance Treaty when Bismarck was forced to step down. **Craig** (1981) has written that 'Bismarck could take satisfaction in the fact that the network of alliances was still in good repair and indeed had been strengthened by Great Britain's association with the Triple Alliance. There was no immediate prospect of new troubles in Europe.'

All of Bismarck's foreign policy objectives from 1871 had, therefore, been achieved. Historians are divided, however, in their judgements of Bismarck's achievements. **Langer** (1931) argued that 'no other statesman of Bismarck's standing had ever before shown the same great moderation and sound political sense of the possible and the desirable'. Recent historians have tended to be more critical in their judgements. **Waller** (1974) has pointed out that 'the preservation of peace was more a result of the good sense and moderation of others' than the skill shown by Bismarck. **Craig** (1981) has described Bismarck's approach to diplomacy as 'expediency rather than creativity' and has pointed out that 'even before his successors abandoned it, his alliance system was on the point of collapse because of the irreconcilable conflict of interest between Austria and Russia in the Balkan peninsula'.

In order to make a reasoned judgement on the success or failure of Bismarck's foreign policy we have to understand the context within which he was working and his own approach to the challenges he faced. Although he had responsibility for German foreign policy he was not a completely free agent since he had always to convince the Kaiser of the soundness of his policies and he had to be aware of domestic political pressures. He was dealing with foreign governments which were themselves subject to their own political pressures and whose responses, therefore, could not always be predicted with any certainty. Bismarck saw international relations as an exercise in Realpolitik; it was his task to discern the possibilities for Germany within any given situation and to make best use of them. Problems in international relations were, for Bismarck, not capable of being solved in the long term and the best that could be achieved was to manage those problems to Germany's best advantage. He had nothing but contempt for more idealistic approaches to international relations, such as the English statesman Gladstone's belief in a '**Concert of Europe**'. Bismarck had a narrow, sceptical, limited concept of foreign policy and within those terms he was undoubtedly successful. His successors, however, were unable to manage the alliance system which he bequeathed to them. This was partly due to their own limited understanding of the complexity of that system and partly because the alliances were unsustainable in the long term.

KEY TERM

Concert of Europe After the Congress of Vienna in 1815 the European powers held congresses on a number of occasions as a means of resolving disputes and maintaining or adjusting the balance of power. Statesmen like Gladstone regarded this Concert of Europe approach as being preferable to war and as a way of avoiding the division of Europe into rival alliances. The last congress was held in Berlin in 1884 to resolve colonial disputes in Africa.

SECTION 5

What was Bismarck's legacy?

KEY POINTS

Bismarck's successors were conspicuously unable to manage the political system which he had bequeathed to them with the same success as Bismarck; his alliance system fell apart in their hands. Interpretation of this situation focuses on two points.

- Was the legacy itself seriously flawed and doomed to fail because of its inherent contradictions?
- Were Bismarck's successors simply unequal to the task confronting them?

HISTORICAL INTERPRETATION

As with most major historical figures, Bismarck inspired controversy both among his contemporaries and between historians who have written about this period of German history. In his own lifetime and after his death he was regarded as a national icon by millions of Germans who regarded him as the architect of German unification. Yet many from his own class, the Prussian Junker landowners, regarded him as a dangerous subversive. Historians, also, have been unable to agree about his place in German history. For some he was an arch-conservative who was dedicated to preserving the power of the old elite and of the Prussian monarchy whilst for others he was a great moderniser, responsible for far-reaching political, social and economic change in Germany.

CHANGES IN GERMANY

It is undeniable that Germany underwent greater change, while Bismarck was Minister-President of Prussia and Imperial Chancellor, than any other European country in the same period. When he entered office in 1862 Germany was a collection of states of varying sizes, loosely linked together in the German Confederation. Austria was the dominant power in that Confederation. Some German states had constitutions in 1862 which allowed differing degrees of power to their parliamentary institutions, but there were no national political institutions and no national political parties. Economically, Germany was beginning to experience industrialisation and the growth of internal and external trade but still lagged behind the most advanced industrial economy, Great Britain. Socially, Germany was still largely a rural, agrarian society in which the aristocratic landowners held sway and the members of the small but growing middle class were no more than junior partners. By 1890 much had changed. Germany was a unified state with 'modern' political institutions such as a Reichstag elected on the basis of universal manhood suffrage. There were national institutions and national parties. Germany had taken its place as one of five great powers in Europe, occupying a central position on the continent, with a large, modern, well-equipped army and a strong industrial base to supply that army's needs. An overseas empire placed Germany alongside Britain and France as one of the major forces in international affairs. The German economy had expanded and diversified and Germany was now in a position to challenge the pre-eminence of British manufacturers in export markets.

These were solid achievements. It would be stretching credulity to attribute the credit for all of them to Bismarck alone. He was undoubtedly a 'great man' and his policies made a major contribution to the advances made by Germany in this period, but he was working within a given political, social and economic framework. German unification would probably have occurred without Bismarck but its timing and the shape of the German Reich which was actually created in 1871 owed a great deal to him. As **Carr** (1987) has put it, Bismarck was 'the executant of a historical process'. Although the 'heroic' view of Bismarck, in which he was regarded as the puppet-master who was pulling all the strings and shaping the destiny of Germany, is no longer given serious credence by historians, it would be fair to say that he exercised a major influence on the development of Germany and that he deserves credit for the positive achievements as well as criticism for the failures.

A LEGACY OF PROBLEMS

There was much in his legacy which caused problems for his successors. German society was deeply divided and the divisions were beginning to cause serious political problems. **Williamson** (1986) has argued that even the most gifted statesman would have found the legacy difficult because industrialisation was creating tensions which were virtually insoluble within the existing constitutional framework. The growth of the working class and the rise of socialism were developments which were viewed with alarm by the Prussian aristocratic–monarchical forces which were firmly entrenched within the power structures of the German state. **Craig** (1981) has described Bismarck's constitutional settlement of 1871 as an 'anachronistic political system in which he had sought to stifle every progressive tendency'. Once again, Bismarck has been charged with having no long-term solutions for the problems of the German Reich. His responses were sometimes brilliant, but essentially negative, expedients.

BISMARCK'S RESPONSIBILITY

The fact that Bismarck's successors were not capable of meeting the challenges they faced in both domestic and foreign affairs is a failing for which Bismarck has been blamed. A number of historians, including **Carr** (1987), have argued that, in depriving the Reichstag of genuine power and treating it on occasions with contempt, he kept the best minds out of politics. He made no attempt to train a political class or to prepare a successor. His approach was to attempt to satisfy the material demands of the different classes, but he obstructed the development of a more responsible government in which power would be shared between the monarch and his ministers on the one hand and the parliamentary institutions on the other. This is the basis of the charge that he retarded Germany's political development. **Carr** quotes the sociologist Max Weber (1917) in support of this view. 'Bismarck left behind him', wrote Weber, 'a nation without any political education . . . Above all, he left behind a nation without any political will, accustomed to allow the great statesman at its head to look after its policy for it.' If Bismarck's successors were

1245

A cartoon from Punch, called 'Dropping the Pilot', drawn in March 1890.

politically inexperienced and inept, Bismarck himself can be blamed for presiding over a political system which denied able people the chance to gain experience and develop their talents.

THE 'BISMARCK DEBATE'

These are serious charges but it is important that we acknowledge the degree of controversy which surrounds Bismarck, even after so much time has elapsed since his retirement. There have been a number of biographies and other studies of German history during the past twenty years and, far from bringing the debate to a conclusion, the historians involved have opened up new areas of controversy. **Waller** (1991) has challenged the view that German society was lacking in political development. He points out that imperial Germany was, in many ways, quite 'liberal' and 'modern'. Parliamentary life and public debate were vigorous. The Reichstag had some power and it was elected on the basis of universal manhood suffrage. Each state had its own constitution and its own *Landtag*. The result of this was that, by 1890, Germany had many more men who were experienced in political activity than Great Britain. He goes on to assert: 'Considering that education was better in Germany, it is probably true that political awareness was greater there than in Britain.' Perhaps the strength of the German SPD by 1890, in comparison with the slow and hesitant development of socialist parties in Britain, France and elsewhere is an indication of the greater political awareness in Germany.

The conservative structure of the constitution and the entrenched power of the Prussian aristocracy were undoubtedly a barrier to reform and to the accommodation of new political and social forces within the framework of the Reich. It is important to acknowledge, however, that the National Liberals, who were the main progressive party in German politics until the 1880s, achieved virtually all the reform they wanted from the imperial constitution of 1871. Apart from their clash with Bismarck over parliamentary control of the military budget, the powers granted to the Reichstag were broadly in line with their expectations. The constitution was a compromise between aristocratic and monarchical elements on the one hand and democratic and constitutional forces on the other and, as such, it was broadly acceptable to most Germans.

But was it what Bismarck wanted? Here again there has been sharp disagreement between historians. One school of thought, associated with the German historian **Lothar Gall** (1986), sees Bismarck as a Prussian conservative who, in the process of expanding Prussian power, had unleashed forces which he was then unable to control. These forces – nationalism, liberalism, economic modernisation – brought about a radical transformation of German society with which Bismarck was increasingly at odds. Thus in the 1880s he tried to slow down the pace of reform and to suppress those elements which were attempting to undermine the traditional conservative forces. This interpretation sees Bismarck not as the master tactician but as an inept bungler who, in the last years of his chancellorship, was making increasingly desperate efforts to defend the indefensible.

Bismarck can be portrayed as a conservative Prussian or a liberal moderniser, and as a master of the political situation or, in the words of **Gall**, a 'sorcerer's apprentice'. His contemporaries could not agree about him and neither can historians. This is partly because the man himself had such a complex character with many contradictions and partly because his work and achievements over such a long period contain many, apparently contradictory, elements. The Germany he left behind was in many ways a state as 'modern' as any in Europe at that time but it also displayed strikingly traditional and conservative features. Bismarck's Germany will continue to be a subject of lively debate among historians and there is much scope for students of history to engage with that debate.

Whether Bismarck's successors were unequal to their task is not a question which falls within the scope of this book. The question of whether his legacy contained serious flaws is a matter on which there is no consensus among historians. The fact that he himself was having increasing difficulty in managing the political system during the 1880s shows that his legacy certainly contained the potential to cause problems for his successors. These flaws in the political system can be summarised as follows:
- An authoritarian constitution which was not adapted to take account of the changing social and economic realities in Germany.
- A constitution which gave the Kaiser sole responsibility for appointing and dismissing the Chancellor. In the hands of the unstable and irrational Wilhelm II this left his chancellors subject to his changing whims.
- By denying the Reichstag a positive role in shaping policy and framing the laws, Bismarck's constitution encouraged a confrontational relationship between government and Reichstag. In the years before 1914 this conflict threatened to make Germany ungovernable.
- Bismarck's tendency to exacerbate divisions by persecuting 'Reichsfeinde' – Catholics, Poles, socialists – soured the atmosphere of the Reich and set a pattern which was continued after 1890.
- By enshrining the special status of the army in the constitution and allowing the army to have political independence, Bismarck bequeathed to his successors a position in which the army General Staff interfered in the formulation of foreign policy.

A2 ASSESSMENT: GERMANY 1848–90

SOURCES QUESTIONS IN THE STYLE OF OCR

Read Sources A to D and answer the following questions. You may also use your own knowledge to help you to answer the questions.

> 1 Account for the differences between Sources B and C on Bismarck's aims during the crisis over the Hohenzollern candidature in 1870.

> 2 What do Sources A to D tell us about Bismarck's role in bringing about the Franco-Prussian war of 1870–1?

Source A
(Bismarck comments on the diplomatic crisis which resulted from the premature publication of the news of the Hohenzollern candidature.)

We have in fact no intention of interfering in Spanish affairs and there is no question of our support when Prussia has no concern in the matter. If France wants to interfere that is her business, if she wants to make war on us because the Spaniards elect a German as a King, it would be quite unjustifiably quarrelsomeness. We shall never wage a war of the Spanish succession and the whole ado is premature as long as the Cortes (Spanish Parliament) have not voted. Should the French attack us, however, we shall of course resist.

Bismarck to the Prussian Ambassador in London, July 1870.

Source B
(A twentieth-century British historian denies that Bismarck planned the war.)

There is a simple defence of Bismarck's policy in 1870: he did not provoke war at all, except in the narrowest sense of exploding it at the last moment. Later on, when the war had become a national legend, Bismarck tried to take the credit for it; but it was unearned. Of course the Hohenzollern candidature was of his making. Its object was to act as a check on France, not to provoke her into war. His encouragement of or indifference towards the Spanish affair varied inversely with Franco-Russian entente. But the candidature was primarily not a move in foreign policy at all. Bismarck's overriding concern was with southern Germany; and a Hohenzollern on the Spanish throne was designed to raise Prussian prestige south of the Main.

A.J.P.Taylor, *Bismarck and Europe*, 1952.

Source C

(A twentieth-century American historian of German origin sees Bismarck as having a major responsibility for starting the war.)

What did Bismarck intend to achieve with the Hohenzollern candidature? The known evidence does not provide a conclusive answer. In none is there any direct proof that the chancellor expected war to develop out of the Spanish affair. Nor do the documents show absolutely what he expected to achieve if his end were not war. The answer must be reasoned from the general situation, his actions and what we know of his political technique.

Clearly the Hohenzollern candidacy was an offensive act. It is false to claim that his aim in May (1870) was to gain an ally for the coming crisis with France. He deliberately set sail on a collision course (with France) with the intent of provoking either war or a French internal collapse. The partisans of his innocence ask us to believe a most improbable case: that the shrewdest diplomatic mind of recent history permitted Germany to be drawn into a war which he was eager to avoid. The man who in 1863, 1865 and 1867 had known how to approach the brink and yet save the peace when it was wise to do so found it impossible to manoeuvre his way out of a situation of his own making in the summer of 1870 without resort to violence.

O. Pflanze, *Bismarck and the Development of Germany*, 1963.

Source D

(A twentieth-century German historian argues that Bismarck was willing to go to war.)

In July 1870 each side (Prussia and France) tried to outdo each other. To an unimportant though foolish French demand Bismarck replied with a statement that to our violent age seems almost laughably harmless. The French regime wanted a cheap humiliation of Prussia or, if that was impossible, war. Bismarck almost certainly preferred war to such a humiliation; particularly as he regarded war as inevitable anyway and because it would open up a satisfactory avenue along which he could pursue policies which would otherwise reach a dead end. For the attainment of the Prussian goal, the establishment of a 'little' Germany, no war against France was or should have been necessary.

G. Mann, *The History of Germany since 1789*, 1968.

Reading
You will need to read Section 2 (pages 107–122). You will also find it useful to read Chapter 4 (pages 35–49).

How to answer these questions
Question 1
The question is asking you both to identify and to explain the differences between these two sources. At first sight the differences are obvious: Source B says that Bismarck did not intend to provoke war; Source C says that he did. But on closer inspection you should be able to find that the differences between the sources are less clear-cut. A full explanation of the differences will be necessary to achieve higher marks.

The question asks you to 'account for' the differences. This can be done in a number of ways.

- Use all four sources by cross-referencing between them to show how the evidence is inconclusive and leaves scope for historians to interpret it in a variety of ways.
- Refer to the authors of these two sources: what conclusions, if any, may be drawn from the fact that one is a British historian and the other an American (of German origin)?
- Use your background knowledge of the subject to place the sources in context. What do you know about Bismarck's aims, methods and actions which would help you to understand how different historians can reach different conclusions about his responsibility for the war against France?
- Note that the question does not ask you to take sides in this controversy, You are asked only to explain the differences in interpretation.

Question 2
The question is asking you both to summarise the main conclusions of all four sources and to evaluate the role of Bismarck in the outbreak of the Franco-Prussian war. The key question at issue here is whether Bismarck played the leading role in bringing about the war. The sources differ on this point. What are the main differences? As with Question 1, there are some finer points of interpretation which you should look for and include in your answer.

- How honest do you think Bismarck was being in Source A?
- What is the author of Source B referring to when he writes, 'Later on, when the war had become a national legend . . .'?
- How significant is the author of Source C's admission that 'The known evidence does not provide a conclusive answer'?
- Is Source D more balanced than the others? How does this affect its reliability?

Having analysed the sources you should place them into context. How important was Bismarck in bringing about the Franco-Prussian war? You will need to explain the situation in Germany in the late 1860s, the position of the southern states, French policy and the actions of the French government at this time as well as Bismarck's own policies and his methods. It would be helpful if you were able to refer to the works of other historians with which you are familiar, especially if you are aiming for the highest marks.

ESSAY QUESTIONS

To gain the highest marks in essay questions you will need to do the following:

Analyse throughout the essay
This can be done by making sure that you plan a line of argument before you start the writing. At the start of each paragraph you must make the next point of your argument, explain it and then use evidence to support your point. Always keep the question in mind, particularly the key words within the question. These will act as a reference point to help you keep the argument relevant.

To help you keep your analysis flowing, start each paragraph with words that lead into an argument. Some examples of these are:

The most important reason is . . .
Another key point is that . . .
In contrast with . . .
One of the most significant consequences was . . .

Support your argument by using well selected evidence
The factual examples you give must be accurate and relevant to the point you are trying to make. Give enough factual detail to make clear how the factual example relates to the point you are making but do not allow yourself to drift into irrelevant narrative. The lack of any factual example will reduce your argument to the level of an 'unsupported assertion' which will earn very few marks at all.

Make a clear and consistent attempt to reach a judgement
In your essay you must argue throughout. You must reflect on the evidence you have given and make points which answer the question directly. Your conclusion must be consistent with the arguments you have developed through your essay.

Show evidence of independent thought

You do not have to be original. Independent thought means that you have reflected on what you have read in books and that you can explain the ideas you have picked up in your own words.

Refer to the works of historians you have read

You are expected to be familiar with the different interpretations put forward by historians and aware that many aspects of the subject are controversial. This should be reflected in your arguments.

Language skills

It is essential that you write in paragraphs and that your grammar is accurate. Learn the correct spellings of key people and places.

Question 1

> Which was the most important principle on which the German Reich of 1871 was founded: liberalism, nationalism or Prussian conservatism?

Reading

To help you answer this question you should read Sections 2 and 3 and Chapters 1, 3, 5 and 6 of the AS section.

Key words

Always approach an essay question by first identifying the key words. In this case they are 'most important principle', 'Reich . . . was founded'. These should act as signposts to help you plan your answer and check for relevance.

Plan

At the outset, get clear in your mind what your main line of argument will be. This can be called the 'key theme' of your answer. In this case, your key theme might be as follows:

liberalism and nationalism each made a contribution to the shaping of the institutions and policies of the Reich but ultimate power still rested with Prussian conservative forces, that is

the monarchy,

the Junker aristocracy,

the army.

Having outlined your key theme you can then begin to plan your paragraph structure. Bear in mind that a question like this requires treatment of all three factors with some comparison between them, although you do not have to devote equal amounts of time or space to each of them. Comparisons work best if you use a point-by-point approach although you may prefer to deal with each factor in turn; if you follow the latter approach, be sure to keep the comparison going throughout the essay.

Writing

In your answer you need to include the following:

- The development of the National Liberal movement in Germany, through the 1848 revolutions and the foundation of the Nationalverein. The strengths and weaknesses of this movement.
- The strength of conservative forces in Germany, particularly in Prussia, and the role that Prussia played in the unification of Germany.
- The position and beliefs of Bismarck. Where did he stand in relation to Prussian conservatism (was he a typical Junker?).
- The constitution of the German Reich. Which elements in the constitution reflected the influence of nationalism and which showed the influence of conservatism?
- The economic policies of the Reich. How far did these follow the liberal agenda?
- References to the works of any historians which you have read.

Question 2

How successfully did the government of the German Reich deal with internal opposition in the years 1871–90?

Reading

You will need to read Section 3 of the A2 section of this book, together with Chapters 5 and 7 of the AS section.

Key words

The key words in this question are: 'how successfully', 'government', 'deal with internal opposition'.

Plan

The focus of this answer should be on the policies which Bismarck adopted to counter internal opposition and how successful these policies were. Most of the answer will be devoted to the Kulturkampf and the anti-socialist campaign. A possible key theme is as follows: neither the Kulturkampf nor the anti-socialist campaign succeeded in suppressing the opposition, although Bismarck enjoyed some short-term success in containing the growth of the socialist movement in the early 1880s.

Writing

In your answer you should include the following:

- The nature and extent of the opposition to the Reich from Catholics, with particular reference to the Centre party.
- Bismarck's Kulturkampf. The policies which were adopted to weaken the influence of the Catholic church.
- The success of the policy, as reflected in such indicators as election results.
- The nature and extent of the opposition from the socialists.
- Bismarck's anti-socialist policies, both in the form of repressive laws and of 'state socialism'.
- The success or failure of these policies, as reflected in election results and so on.
- Opposition from other sources, such as national minorities.
- References to the works of any historians that you have read.

Question 3

To what extent was the annexation of Alsace–Lorraine the main cause of Germany's difficulties in foreign policy in the years 1871–90?

Reading

To answer this question you will need to read Section 4 together with Chapter 8 of the AS section.

Key words

The key words in this question are: 'to what extent', 'annexation of Alsace –Lorraine', 'main cause of difficulties'. The question is therefore asking you to evaluate the extent to which the problems in foreign policy stemmed from the decision to annex Alsace–Lorraine.

Plan

The focus of this answer will be on the problems which Bismarck had to deal with in his conduct of foreign policy throughout this period. There is so much material to be included in this essay that selection and organisation will be critical. A chronological approach may be appropriate, especially if you divide the period up into phases, such as pre- and post-1879. Analytical answers, however, are usually more successful when planned on a point-by-point basis. In this case you could deal with the question on a problem-by-problem or a country-by-country basis.

A possible key theme would be: the annexation of Alsace–Lorraine left a legacy of French bitterness which could lead to a future war unless Bismarck could succeed in keeping France isolated; this affected his relations with other powers, but there were other problems which faced German foreign policy, especially in the 1880s.

Writing

In your answer you must include the following:

- Bismarck's aims in foreign policy, especially his priority of keeping France isolated.
- The significance of the annexation of Alsace–Lorraine for both France and Germany.
- The implementation of Bismarck's policies in the period 1871–9, with particular reference to the alliance systems. How far were his policies towards Austria–Hungary and Russia influenced by the aim of keeping France isolated?
- The development of foreign policy after the Dual Alliance and the difficulties of maintaining good relations with both Austria–Hungary and Russia at the same time. How far were these difficulties the result of other problems?
- The development of relations with France, particularly the closer relationship which developed in the early to mid-1880s through colonial expansion.
- References to the works on this subject by historians that you have read.

BIBLIOGRAPHY

WORKS PARTICULARLY RELEVANT TO AS STUDENTS

Berghohn, V. *Modern Germany: Society, Economy and Politics in the twentieth century*, Cambridge University Press, 1982

Blackbourn, D. *The Fontana History of Germany 1815–1918*, HarperCollins, 1991

Breuilly, J. *The Formation of the First German Nation State, 1800–71*, Macmillan, 1996

Röhl, J. C. G. *The Kaiser and His Court – Wilhelm II and the Government of Germany*, Cambridge University Press, 1996

Stiles, A. *The Unification of Germany*, Hodder & Stoughton, 1989

Wehler, H. A. *The German Empire, 1871–1918*, Leamington Spa, 1985

Williamson, D. *Bismarck and Germany, 1862–90*, Longman, 1986

WORKS PARTICULARLY RELEVANT TO A2 STUDENTS

Blackbourn, D. *The Fontana History of Germany 1815–1918*, HarperCollins, 1991

Breuilly, J. *The Formation of the First German Nation State, 1800–71*, Macmillan, 1996

Carr, W. *A History of Germany, 1815–1985*, Hodder & Stoughton, 1987

Craig, G. *Germany 1866–1945*, Oxford University Press, 1981

Eyck, E. *Bismarck and the German Empire*, Allen & Unwin, 1950

Gall, L. *Bismarck – The White Revolutionary*, Allen & Unwin, 1986

Grenville, J. *Europe Re-shaped, 1848–78*, Fontana/Collins, 1976

Hargreaves, D. *Bismarck and German Unification*, Macmillan, 1991

Henderson, W. O. *The Rise of German Industrial Power*, Temple Smith, 1975

John, M. 'The Unification of Germany: The View from Below', *Modern History Review*, April 1991

Langer, B. *European Alliances and Alignments, 1871–1890*, Knoff, 1931

Pflanze, O. *Bismarck and the Development of Germany. The Period of Unification, 1815–71*, Princeton, 1963

Roberts, J. *Europe 1880–1945*, Longman, 1989

Stiles, A. *The Unification of Germany*, Hodder & Stoughton, 1989

Stone, N. *Europe Transformed, 1878–1919*, HarperCollins, 1985

Taylor, A.J.P. *The Course of German History*, Methuen, 1961

Waller, W. *Bismarck at the Crossroads*, Athlone Press, 1974

Waller, W. 'The Enigma of Bismarck as Imperial Chancellor', *Modern History Review*, February 1991

Williamson, D. *Bismarck and Germany, 1862–90*, Longman, 1986

INDEX

Africa 83, 98, 161, 162, 165–6
agriculture 6–7, 57, 59, 63, 64, 66–7, 92, 94, 122–3, 153
Alexander III, Tsar of Russia 82, 162
Alsace-Lorraine 48, 149, 161
anti-Semitism 68, 72
aristocracy 6, 9–10, 27–8, 52, 65
  see also Junkers
army 18, 29, 31–3, 65, 95, 100, 102, 132–35, 148, 154
artisans see Handwerker
Ausgleich 136
Austria-Hungary 75, 76–7, 136
  Balkans 78–82, 83, 162–4
  Dual Alliance 80–1, 159, 160, 163, 164–5
Austrian Empire 3, 5
  Austro-Prussian war 40–3, 131, 132, 134–7, 140, 164
  constitution of 1849 21–2, 23
  Erfurt Union 26–7
  German Confederation 11–12, 36–7
  Prussia 30–1
  revolutions 1848 14, 17–18, 118–19, 120–1
  Schleswig-Holstein 16, 37–41, 129, 138–9
  unification of Germany 35–6, 142–3
  war with France (1859) 30–1, 32, 132, 140
  Zollverein 12, 30, 129–31, 136
Austro-Prussian war (1866) 40–3, 131, 132, 134–7, 140, 164

Baden 3, 6, 14, 23, 48, 124
Balkans 76–7, 78–82, 162–4
Bavaria 6, 14, 23, 26–7, 48, 52, 98, 125, 131, 144–5
Bebel, August 69, 70, 72
Bennigsen, Rudolf von 31, 58, 150
Berlin Conference (1885) 161
Berlin, Treaty of (1878) 80, 162
Bethmann Hollweg, von 99, 101

Bismarck, Otto von
  army 154
  constitutional crisis 1862 33–4
  Crimean war 30
  fall of 86–8, 89
  foreign policy 75–84, 157–67
  Kulturkampf 53–6, 57–8, 149–50
  North German Confederation 43–4
  Schleswig-Holstein crisis 37–41, 134, 139–40
  social change 153–6
  socialism 69–74, 86–7, 149, 152, 154–5
  unification 35–49, 127, 137–42, 147–50
Bohemia 21–2, 118, 121
Bosnia and Herzegovina 78, 80, 81
Boulanger, General 161–2
Bulgaria 78–80, 82, 83, 154, 163–4
Bulow, Count Bernard von 92, 96, 97–9
Bundesrat 43, 50, 144
Bundestag see Federal Diet

Caprivi, General Leo von 94
Centre party 54–5, 57–8, 59, 146, 149–50, 155
colonial empire 82–3, 161, 165–6
Conservative party 57, 59, 87, 125, 146, 155
constitution of 1849 20–3, 119–21
constitution of 1871 50–3, 144–7, 153–4
Crimean war 30, 142

Denmark 11, 16–17, 37–8, 120, 132, 139–40
Dreikaiserbund (Three Emperors' League) 76–7, 81, 160, 162, 164
Dual Alliance (1879) 80–1, 83, 159, 160, 162–3, 164–5

economy 28–9, 56–9, 122, 153
education 152
Ems telegram 47

Erfurt Union 26–7, 138
Eulenberg, Philipp von 89, 97

Falk, Adalbert 53, 55
Federal Diet (*Bundestag*) 6, 26–7, 35, 40, 145
Ferdinand, Emperor of Austria 5, 17–18, 125
Flottenpolitik 96
foreign policy 75–84, 157–67
France 75–8, 83–4, 161–2
  Austro-Prussian war 134
  colonialism 83, 166
  Franco-Prussian war 46–8, 69, 133–34, 135, 140–1
  isolation 46, 158, 160, 161
  revolution 1848 118
  Schleswig-Holstein crisis 40
  unification of Germany 35–6
  war with Austria (1859) 30, 32, 132, 140
Franco-Prussian war (1870-71) 46–9, 69, 133–34, 135, 140–1
Frankfurt Parliament 14–17, 20–3, 27, 117–22, 124
Frankfurt, Peace of (1871) 48
Franz Josef, Emperor 18, 39, 75, 125, 135, 136–7
Frederick, Duke of Augustenberg 37–9, 129
Free Conservative party 43, 59, 87, 146, 155
Friedrich Wilhelm III, King of Prussia 11
Friedrich Wilhelm IV, King of Prussia 12, 13, 14, 17, 19–20, 23, 25–7, 30–1, 118–19, 124, 125
'Fundamental Rights of the German People' 27, 117, 119, 120

Gagern, Heinrich von 16
Gastein, Convention of (1865) 39–40
German Confederation 3–4, 6, 16–17, 26–7, 36–7, 41, 130, 131, 138, 140
German Social Democratic party (SPD) 71–4, 87, 92–4, 98, 101, 146, 152, 154–5
Great Britain 40, 77, 80, 82–3, 134, 142, 159, 161, 165–6

Grossdeutsch 21–2, 129

Handwerker 9, 119, 122, 123, 124, 125
Hanover 23, 26, 41, 130, 131, 135, 149
Hecker, Friedrich von 120
Hesse-Cassel 6, 27, 28, 41
Hollweg *see Bethmann Hollweg*
Hungary 18, 21, 136

industry 3, 8–10, 28–9, 59, 61–3, 90–1, 123–4, 132, 151, 153
Italy 30, 40, 41, 46, 77, 82, 134, 136, 140, 160

Junkers 6, 52, 57, 65, 66, 88, 105

Kaiser 22–3, 50–1, 153–4
Kartell 87, 155, 162
Kleindeutsch 21–2, 50
Kulturkampf 53–6, 57–8, 149–50

Landrat 66
Lassalle, Ferdinand 70
Leo XIII, Pope 55
Leopold, Prince 47
liberalism 10, 59, 97, 119–22, 126, 146–7
Liebknecht, Karl 70, 72
London Conference (1867) 46
London, Treaty of (1852) 37–8, 134, 139
Louis Philippe, King of France 14, 118
Ludwig I, King of Bavaria 52, 125
Luxembourg 45–6

Marx, Karl 69, 70, 117, 124
Mediterranean Agreements (1887) 84, 160, 163, 166
Metternich, Prince Clemens von 3, 5, 7, 14, 17, 118
middle class 9–10, 64–5, 151
Mittelstand 67, 102
Moltke, Count Helmut von 41, 133, 134–5
Montenegro 78

Napoleon III, Emperor of France 40, 41, 44–6, 75, 141

National Liberal party 42, 45, 52–4, 57–9, 87, 146, 148, 149–50, 154
nationalism 10–11, 21, 121, 128–9, 138, 146
Nationalverein 31, 128, 129, 138
Navy 96–7, 105
North German Confederation 41, 42, 43–4, 140

Olmutz Declaration 27, 138

Pan-Slavism 78
particularism 4, 143, 145
peasants 6–7, 28, 63, 64, 66–7, 119–20, 122–3, 125–6, 151–2
Pius IX, Pope 7, 54, 55, 58, 149–50
Poland 21, 36, 149
Posen 21, 121
Prague, Peace of (1866) 41
princes 5–6, 98, 124–5, 144
Progressive party 32–3, 60, 87
Prussia
  aristocracy 6
  army 31–4, 132–35, 148
  Austro-Prussian war 40–3, 131, 132, 134–7, 140, 164
  conservatism 148
  constitution of 1849 21–3, 125–6
  constitutional crisis 1862 31–4
  Erfurt Union 26–7
  France 44–9
  German unification 50, 127–42
  industrialisation 29
  Parliament 99
  revolution 1848 14, 19–20, 25–6, 118, 120–2, 124, 125–6
  Schleswig-Holstein 16–17, 37–41, 129
  School Bill, 1892 95
  socialism 72
  unification of Germany 35–49, 127–42, 145
  Zollverein 11–13, 30

Radical party 87
Radowitz, Joseph von 26, 27
railways 8–9, 29, 131–2

Realpolitik 34, 137–8
Reichstag 22–3, 43–4, 51–2, 58–9, 69, 92, 95, 98, 101–2, 145–7, 148, 153
Reinsurance Treaty (1887) 83–4, 87, 160, 163–4, 166
religion 7, 53–6, 149–50, 151–2
revolutions 1848 14–24, 70, 117–26
Rhineland 129–30
Roman Catholic Church 7, 53–6, 149–50, 151
Romania 82, 160
Roon, Albrecht von 32
Russia 30, 36, 40, 76–82, 83–4, 138, 142, 159–60, 162–4, 166

Sammlungspolitik 97, 102, 105, 155
San Stefano, Treaty of (1878) 80
Saxony 3, 23, 26, 41, 135
Schleswig-Holstein 11, 16–17, 21, 37–41, 120, 128–9, 134, 139–40
Schlieffen, count von 95, 100
Schwarzenberg, Prince Felix zu 18, 22, 26, 135
Serbia 78, 82
socialism 58–9, 69–74, 86–7, 92–3, 149, 154–5
Spain 46–7, 141
SPD *see* German Social Democratic party
state socialism 73–4, 155
Stoecker, Adolf 72

take-off 28
tariffs 12, 56–8, 59–60, 63, 153, 154, 162
Three Emperors' Alliance (1881) 81–2, 83, 160, 163
Tirpitz, Admiral von 96
trade 10
  see also tariffs; *Zollverein*
trade unions 71–2, 93
Triple Alliance (1882) 82, 84, 166
Turkey 80

unification 35–50, 127–42, 143–4
universal suffrage 15, 43, 147, 148
urbanisation 63, 64, 151–2

Venetia 120

'War in Sight' crisis (1875) 77–8, 158, 161
Weltpolitik 96, 98, 104
Wilhelm I, Kaiser 32–3, 36–7, 39–40, 47,
 58, 69, 86, 141, 143
Wilhelm II, Kaiser 86–7
 anti-Semitism 103
 army 89
 Bulow, von 97, 99
 character 89–90

First World War 104–5
influence on policy 103, 105
socialists 96
Weltpolitik and *Flottenpolitik* 96–7
Windthorst, Ludwig 54
working class 65, 67, 70–4, 123–4, 151–2,
 155
Wurttemberg 3, 6, 26, 27, 48, 145

Zollverein 11–13, 30, 35, 129–32